CAT COLLECTIBLES

CAT
COLLECTIBLES
PAULINE FLICK

**Wallace-Homestead
Book Company**
Radnor, Pennsylvania

A QUINTET BOOK

First published in the United States by
Wallace-Homestead, a division of the
Chilton Book Company, Radnor, Pennsylvania

ISBN 0-87069-678-5

This book was designed and produced by
Quintet Publishing Limited
6 Blundell Street
London N7 9BH

Creative Director: Richard Dewing
Designers: Annie Moss, James Lawrence
Project Editor: Laura Sandelson
Editor: Maggie McCormick
Photographers: Nick Nicholson,
Harry L. Rinker Jr.

Typeset in Great Britain by
Central Southern Typesetters, Eastbourne
Manufactured in Hong Kong by
Regent Publishing Services Limited
Printed in Hong Kong by
Leefung-Asco Printers Limited

CONTENTS

Introduction 7

CHAPTER ONE   Ceramic cats   13

CHAPTER TWO   Cats as toys   25

CHAPTER THREE   Cats at Christmas and other festivals   45

CHAPTER FOUR   Cats through the post   55

CHAPTER FIVE   Wooden cats   63

CHAPTER SIX   Metal cats   71

CHAPTER SEVEN   Cats in textiles   79

CHAPTER EIGHT   Glass cats   87

CHAPTER NINE   Cats in advertising   91

CHAPTER TEN   Kitchen cats   99

CHAPTER ELEVEN   Character cats   107

CHAPTER TWELVE   Various cats   117

Price guide   124

Bibliography and Collector's Clubs   126

Index   128

INTRODUCTION

— 1 —

A jolly Cat-in-the-Box
toy from Europe,
possibly Germany,
was probably made
between 1900 and
1925. It measures
$3^{3}/_{16}$in $\times$ $3^{1}/_{4}$in
$\times$ $3^{3}/_{8}$in.

Many cat-lovers lay the foundation of an interesting collection almost by accident. Usually it begins with keeping a real pet – whether it is a pedigree or rescued stray hardly seems to matter. Under the spell of one of these little animals, the enthusiast becomes aware of an enormous number of cat-related artifacts, and a few random purchases are made. My own collection, I realize now, was inspired by a colony of feral cats I used to feed in London. Some of them were tame enough to move in with me, whereupon friends took to sending appropriate cards for Christmas and birthdays, and I began to cut out newspaper reports of feline adventures, of rescues from high roofs or deep holes, of incredible journeys back to old homes, and of cats living to a great age or growing exceptionally fat. I saw beautiful porcelain models in museums, compared them with others in auction houses and specialist shops, read everything I could find on the subject, and then realized that the scope of cat-collecting is boundless. Not everybody, perhaps, would actually want to possess a mummified cat from ancient Egypt, and many people are

equally squeamish about the creations of the famous Victorian taxidermist William Potter, whose tableaux include a group of stuffed kittens elaborately dressed for a wedding. Probably the best place for such esoteric items is in a museum, but there are hundreds of other strange and wonderful cats that would not seem out of place in a private collection.

The majority of private collections are eventually dispersed, and individual items find new owners. One remarkable exception is the feline menagerie built up by Mrs. Blanche Langton in the 1920s. When she got married, Mrs. Langton, one of ten children of an English clergyman (it is nice to think of pet cats being kept at the Rectory) moved to London, where she found most of the superb models that became known as her "AD" collection; later she and her husband spent some time in Egypt, where they bought the "BC" cats, dating from the pre-Christian era. In 1972 Mrs. Langton generously presented her collection of 94 "AD" cats to Norwich Castle Museum in England, while the "BC" Egyptian cats were given to University College, London. The Norwich treasures range from a

A cat with two kittens, carved from topaz and made in Russia in about 1880. The height is 2¼in.

— 3 —

These two jade cats, beige with dark markings, lie in curled-up attitudes. They are Chinese, probably 16th century. The height is 1in.

small Roman bronze to rare creatures from China and Japan and a galaxy of stars from the great European porcelain factories of the 18th and early 19th centuries, including Meissen, Rockingham, Worcester, and Derby.

In the United States an exceptional private collection was given to the Atkins Museum of Fine Arts in Kansas City by Mr. and Mrs. Frank P. Burnap. Mr. and Mrs. Burnap specialized in early English pottery cats of the period c. 1740–80, robust little figures veined and streaked in agateware and slipware or patterned with a tortoiseshell glaze. Like the Norwich cats, these are important rarities, and comparable models seldom come onto the market today. Those that do are for the connoisseur willing to make a serious investment, but thanks to such generous gifts, collectors can study and enjoy these exquisite cats in museums.

Although ceramic cats form the largest group for collectors, delightful models can be found in many other materials – wood, metal of all kinds, papier-mâché, printed paper and cardboard, glass and textiles. There are useful objects like brass toasting forks with cat handles, doorstops, tea cozies, and even bed linens printed all over with cats. Decorative felines adorn throw pillows and woolwork pictures both old and new, calendars, Christmas trees, and wallpapers. Cat-related toys from bygone nurseries are great favorites with collectors, while printed and embossed paper "scraps" of the late 19th century feature so many cats and kittens that they alone could form a worthwhile collection.

Of course, cats from the past have a special fascination, not only because their numbers are finite and there is the excitement of tracking down some sought-after item, but also because they have an important extra

dimension which puts the continuing story of the animal into its historical context. By the mid-17th century, cats were favored enough for earthenware pitchers to be made in their image; a hundred years later, it was quite usual for artists to include pet cats in children's portraits. Through countless works of art, both great and small, a growing affection and concern for the cat can be traced; and in the second half of the 19th century, this affection had grown into a positive mania, inspiring writers, artists, potters, printers, and far-sighted manufacturers to create the thousands of cat objects so eagerly collected now.

There were many reasons for the Victorian cat's popularity. From a practical point of view, cats were appreciated as catchers of vermin, especially useful in the mills and warehouses of new industrial towns. By 1868 the British postal service was employing official cats to protect the mail; perishable foodstuffs were often sent by mail, and without the efficient cats, a significant number of packages would have been destroyed by rats and mice. Requesting permission from Post Office Headquarters to take on three cats, the Controller of London's Money Order Office pointed out that a penny-halfpenny per day was allowed at the British Museum "and other places of the kind" for each cat, and he suggested that two shillings a week ought to be enough for the care and keep of his three mousers. For almost 120 years, Post Office officials exchanged letters of this kind, requesting and obtaining regular increases in the cats' remuneration. Joyfully, all this correspondence was meticulously filed and has now been brought to light in *Dear Cats: The Post Office Letters*, edited by Russell Ash (Pavilion Books, 1986). To dis-

cover a little book like this, which does so much to set the cat in historical perspective, delights many enthusiasts as much as the purchase of an expensive piece of porcelain.

In addition to their obvious usefulness, cats came to be valued by all classes of society as household pets – companionable, clean, cheap to feed, and good with children. After centuries of cruelty and neglect, they benefited generally from a new and more humane attitude toward all animals, a welcome development resulting in the establishment in Britain and then in other places, of various bodies devoted to animal welfare. The British Society for the Prevention of Cruelty to Animals was founded in 1824; the Battersea Dogs' Home in London, which also takes in stray cats, dates from 1860. Smaller organizations were set up by caring

individuals, and Victorian journals carry numerous reports of animal hospitals and homes for strays.

One of the cat's foremost champions of this period was the British artist Harrison Weir, who illustrated a huge number of animal books as well as writing manuals on cat care. In 1871 he organized the first of many Cat Shows at London's Crystal Palace, and in 1887 he founded the National Cat Club, aimed not only at improving the various breeds, but also at promoting the welfare of non-pedigree animals. When Harrison Weir resigned as president of the Club in 1890, he was succeeded by an even more prolific artist of cat life, and perhaps the most celebrated of all cat-lovers – Louis Wain (1860–1939).

Louis Wain's output was enormous; his work dominates the golden age for collectors, lasting from about

— 4 —

These two late-19th century gift books in decorated bindings were both illustrated by Harrison Weir. *Stories about Cats* was published in 1882, and this edition of *Tales from Catland* in c.1877.

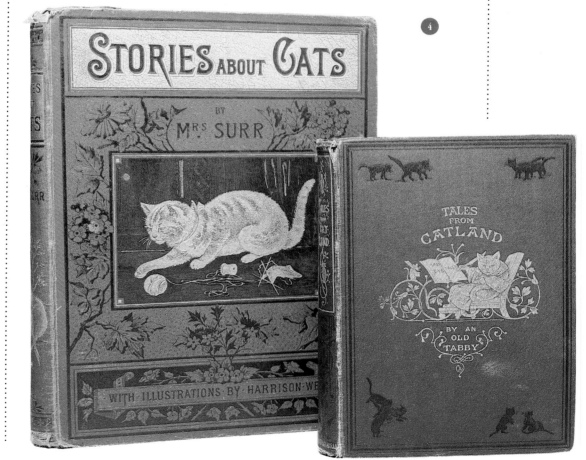

1880 until 1920, and actually defined in postcard-collecting circles as "Catland." In a newspaper article, he explained how fluffy Chinchillas and Persians were what the public looked for in the ideal cat, noting that "with careful breeding the lank body and the long nose disappear, the face becomes condensed . . . into a series of circles." Wain's models have been perfectly described as representing "the well-nourished cat of low metabolism, the sun-faced, smooth-coated tabby of the London doorstep," and the description holds true for all his cats, no matter how anthropo-morphic or caricatured they may be. Every collection ought to include a Louis Wain example; while an original work would be expensive, there are many children's books with his illus-trations and an enormous number of postcards, as well as some excellent

modern reproductions.

The late 19th-century taste for Japanese decoration was reflected in the popularity of cat prints and embroideries from the Far East. Nearer home, the French bronzes of the *animaliers* were increasingly admired, and even the most modest home probably had a German-made cat ornament on the mantel. Lavishly illustrated gift books, souvenirs, Christmas cards, and mechanical toys all featured cats, and all are highly collectible today. So, too, are many of the cat-objects produced in more recent years – the works of various artist-potters, advertising ephemera, museum replicas, postage stamps, and hundreds more.

The problem is that there are just too many collectible cats, and most enthusiasts are forced to specialize. Some confine themselves to Louis

— 5 —

This large Louis Wain print of *The Good Puss* probably hung in an early 20th-century child's bedroom in Great Britain. Note the reference of the "Catsmeat Man," an important person before the days of canned cat food. The width is 27½in.

paper have been added to my collection to bring the story up to date.

Much of the pleasure of collecting is in sharing information with other enthusiasts and in meeting friends at events where cats – real or collectible – are to be seen. Cat Shows and charity bazaars often include stands with very desirable modern cat-objects for sale, and auction houses are holding an increasing number of special "theme" sales devoted to works of art portraying dogs and cats. In the United States, the thriving Cat Collectors' Club held its first national convention in Michigan in the spring of 1992. In England, Salisbury Museum arranged a magnificent exhibition during the winter of 1991/2, displaying cats from all over the world: over 600 of the models on show had been lent from a single private collection, which is still growing. (See appendix for more information on clubs for collectors.)

Sheet music from the musical "The Cat and the Fiddle," with lyrics by the Americans Carleton Lee Colby and Gus Levato of Chicago. It measures 10½in × 13½in.

Wain postcards, or to Felix the Cat, or to heraldic souvenir ware. My own main interest is in anything concerning the Cat and the Fiddle; one theory is that the origin of this strange partnership lies with the Egyptian cat-goddess Bastet and her four-stringed musical instrument, the sistrum. Whether or not this is so, the fiddle-playing cat is certainly shown on early medieval manuscripts; it appears in 14th-century wood-carvings in some English cathedrals in Wells and Hereford, while in a later carving in Yorkshire's Beverley Minster, the feline musician is playing to four kittens. With all these examples, as with some splendid Cat and Fiddle inn signs, I have to be content with photographs, of course, but early nursery-rhyme books, toys, magic-lantern slides, classic illustrations by both Walter Crane and Randolph Caldecott, ceramic models, and wall-

A redware cat by Lester Breininger, 4¾in high, Robesonia, Pennsylvania, made in 1978, is a copy of a 19th-century redware mold.

CERAMIC
CATS

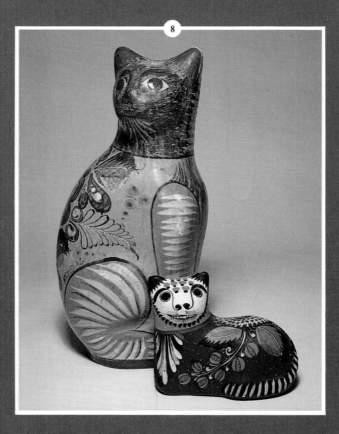

8

— **8** —

Two 20th-century
ceramic cats display
the stylized
decoration typical of
their Mexican origins.

Of all collectible cats, those made from various kinds of ceramic material must be the most numerous and varied. They have been made in virtually every country in the world, and range from delicate Chinese porcelain figures to gaily decorated animals from Mexico. Enthusiasts can spend a fortune on a single perfect specimen of Meissen or Rockingham, or pick up a crested souvenir cat for a trifling sum. Nobody, it seems, ever considers a collection to be complete, and space can always be found for a new acquisition.

A very rich and determined collector might decide to include cats from the 17th century, and search for a piece of Chinese porcelain of the K'ang-Hsi period – perhaps a cat originally made to serve as a lamp or night-light. Something like the blue tabby-marked Persian water container in Mrs. Langton's collection would be equally exotic; London's Victoria and Albert Museum has a similar model, and it is interesting to see how closely these Persian cats resemble the Delft cat pitchers made in England at approximately the same period. The Fitzwilliam Museum in Cambridge, England, has two Lambeth pottery cat pitchers with their dates actually inscribed on the cats' chests – 1657 and 1669.

By the mid-18th century, however, cats of a quite different kind had appeared. By this time, European manufacturers were producing porcelains comparable with the expensive ware exported by the Chinese, and finely modeled figures of humans and animals were made in Germany, France, and England. The famous Meissen factory in Germany made cat figures modeled by J. J. Kaendler, the best-known being the seated pair

— 9 —

This seated cat forms the water container of a "hubble-bubble" pipe measuring 5½in. Made in Persia, possibly in the 17th century, it is painted in underglaze blue with tabby markings.

— 10 —

This sitting 18th-century porcelain cat, 2¼in high, from the great Meissen factory, is painted in enamel colors with patches of brown and black tabby, yellow eyes, and a pink nose.

— 11 —

and known to contemporaries as "toys," include the cat perfume bottle now in New York's Metropolitan Museum that so often appears in photographs; this spotted tabby sits upright, holding a mouse in its right paw and wearing a collar giving its name, Mignonne. Even smaller is a Chelsea seal in the form of a ginger-and-white kitten crouching on a green tasseled pillow, with the underside hollowed out to take a hardstone seal bearing the owner's crest.

REALISTIC CATS
~

In the early years of the 19th century, small realistic cat models were made in England at Rockingham, Derby, Lowestoft, Swansea, Worcester, and by several Staffordshire manufacturers including Charles Bourne of Fenton. Most cats are sitting or crouching, often on a pillow or rounded base. Groups of mothers

— 11 —

A charming fat cat from the Staffordshire porcelain factory of Charles Bourne in Fenton, England. Made between 1817 and 1830, this cat sits on one of the tasseled cushions popular with modelers of this period, and is 2¼in high.

— one cat with a paw raised to its eye, the other holding a mouse up to its mouth – dating from about 1740. Meissen produced many other cats, some as part of a group of figures, or posed among flowers and foliage, but some of the most appealing are the miniatures, such as Mrs. Langton's tiny tabby-and-white, only 2 inches (5.5cm) high. Cats were made at Meissen throughout the 19th century, and they can still be obtained today, although a would-be purchaser might have to wait a long time.

Cats, dogs, monkeys, and squirrels are among the miniature animals to be found on 18th-century porcelain patch-boxes, perfume bottles, and bonbonnières. These exquisite little objects, beautifully modeled and decorated, and with gold or gilt-metal mounts, were made at the French factories at St. Cloud, Mennecy, and Chantilly, and in England at Chelsea and Derby. A ginger cat lying on a Mennecy bonbonnière dates from c.1736–50, while St. Cloud produced an almost identical animal in gray. Chelsea's miniatures, most belonging to the Red Anchor period 1750–60

— 12 —

A seated pair of 19th-century English Staffordshire cats with lustre spots. Such cats were extremely popular in that century as ornaments for the mantlepiece.

— 12 —

An unmarked English porcelain cat and three kittens from the Rockingham factory sit on a tiled rectangular base. A very similar group was produced by Derby, in which one of the kittens is black.

This unmarked group is particularly interesting to students of cat portraiture, as the modeler was obviously familiar with the work of the artist Gottfried Mind (1768–1814). Hungarian by birth, Mind lived and worked in Switzerland, where he specialized almost exclusively in cats and became known as "Der Katzen Raphael," or the Raphael of the Cats. His drawings and paintings were eagerly collected by the rich and fashionable, and reached a wider public through engravings; the little cat family at play (the mother could have been his own favorite, Minette) was published as a lithograph by the London firm of Engelmann Graf Coindet & Co. in 1828. To simplify things, one of the kittens has been left out of the porcelain group, but the whole family appears on a child's transfer-printed plate, c. 1830.

Unless a collector is very knowledgeable, it would be wise to con-

and kittens are very attractive, perhaps none more so than the Rockingham piece of c 1826–30 representing a seated cat with three kittens on a tiled rectangular base. Mrs. Langton's group has the family decorated with tabby patches; but in another version, all the cats are white, the mother wears a collar, and they have been given a saucer of milk. To confuse matters still further, Derby produced an identical model, but the kitten at the rear is black.

Another charming family in Mrs. Langton's collection shows a mother balancing on a stool and playing with her two kittens underneath it.

— 13 —

An engraving, c.1828, based on a painting of a cat with three kittens by Gottfried Mind. A Hungarian living in Switzerland, Mind was very popular and known as the "Raphael of the Cats."

This unmarked porcelain group belongs to the early 19th century. It is interesting to compare this model with Gottfried Mind's picture (below left) which obviously inspired it. It measures 4in.

CHALKWARE CATS
~

On March 10 1768, a Boston newspaper carried an advertisement for "Images, Birds, Cats, Dogs, and all other sorts of curious Animals, all of Plaster-of-Paris." These must have been the ancestors of the chalkware cats of the mid-19th century, simply molded in two sections and varying in height from about five to fifteen inches. At first, these cheerful-looking figures were sized and painted with oil colors, but later ones were decorated with watercolor paints. They were given spots and stripes, and some have neck ribbons or molded collars and bells. Most sit upright, but among the many chalkware cats in New York's Museum of American Folk Art is an unusual example, crouching with a mouse in its mouth.

— 16 —

This seated chalkware cat by an unknown American artist would probably have been made between 1860 and 1900. Its spotted polychrome decoration is typical of chalkware cats. It measures 15½in × 10in. (Abby Aldridge Rockefeller Folk Art Center.)

— 17 —

An American chalkware cat, c.1860–1900 and 15¾in high. Many of these chalkware cats were made in Pennsylvania, but the exact provenance of this attractive model is unknown. (Abby Aldridge Rockefeller Folk Art Center.)

sult an expert before investing in any of these rare porcelain models. Beautiful and desirable as they are, it takes a specialist to point out a cleverly restored ear or paw, to identify an obscure mark, and to cleave a path through the tangle of changing factory names.

EARTHENWARE CATS
~

Another specialized area takes in 18th-century English earthenware cats of the type so well represented in Mr.

and Mrs. Burnap's gift to the Atkins Museum in Kansas City. Because the material is coarser, they are necessarily less finely modeled than the porcelain cats, but many collectors prefer the robust charm of these highly individual animals. Enthusiasts dream of owning one of the rarest of the rare cats made by Thomas Whieldon, the mid-18th century master potter whose name has become synonymous with a whole class of agateware models. Whieldon devised a method of staining white clay

NOTABLE EUROPEAN CATS
~

Such huge numbers of cats have been made during the past century and a half that it is only possible to suggest a few areas of special interest. Most collectors would want to have a representative from Britain's Royal Worcester factory and would probably choose the superb study of a mother cat with her three kittens, modeled by James Hadley and first made in 1875. This piece is unbelievably lifelike, with one kitten playing with the mother's tail, another gazing enquiringly out from under her body, with the third patting her face while she gives it a wash. This is a very rare piece, but it can be seen in Worcester's Dyson Perrins Museum.

Royal Worcester is still making some lovely cats. In 1957 the com-

— 19 —

Pairs of "loving cats" can be found in gift stores all over the world. This couple, with blue and white floral decorations, were made in Thailand, but bought by the owner at a Christmas charity bazaar in 1991. Their heights are 6in and 5½in respectively.

— 18 —

This pair of white glazed porcelain cats, modeled in 1957 by Freda Doughty for the Royal Worcester factory, are more often found decorated in gray or tortoiseshell. The larger is 4in high.

with various metallic oxides and then fusing together layers of different colors; great care was needed when molding this striated clay if the finished product was to have the look of real agate. Striped cats were very successful in this medium, their tabby markings indicated by veining in black, brown, and white. Their poses are uncomplicated; most of them sit upright with head turned sideways and tail wrapped around the body.

The term Whieldon-ware, or more correctly Whieldon-type, is also used to describe cats decorated with a tortoiseshell or marbled glaze. Whieldon developed this method of decorating by sprinkling a plain clay model with various oxides before dipping it into liquid glaze; when fired, the glaze fused with the oxides, giving a rich tortoiseshell finish. A collector hoping to find one of these rare models should go to a reputable dealer.

Later fireplace ornaments from Staffordshire and Sunderland usually portray popular heroes or the familiar "pot dogs" of the spaniel or greyhound type, but pairs of cats were also made. Similar sitting cats were made in the U.S.

pany produced Freda Doughty's models of seven *Alice in Wonderland* characters, including a grinning Cheshire Cat. Only a few were made, but in the same year, two more Freda Doughty cats were issued: a gray Persian (also decorated in ginger) and a short-haired tortoiseshell or gray. These two cats were still in production in the early 1970s, and a good friend who lives in Worcester gave me this charming pair in plain white glazed porcelain, which she had bought at the factory shop in 1991.

James Alder's set of six kittens was issued by Royal Worcester in 1978. In unglazed bisque porcelain, the full set comprises a black-and-white, a ginger, a tabby, a blue Persian, a white Persian, and a Siamese. The company has also produced a set of four "Cats and Kittens" plates designed by Pam Cooper.

A cat designed by the French artist Emile Gallé (1846–1904) would be a colorful addition to any collection. These pottery models of sitting cats, made at Nancy, in France, in the 1880s, are instantly recognizable by their long necks and smiling faces. The most characteristic and best-known are the ones wearing delicately-patterned floral jackets, with "sleeves" fitting over their forelegs and medallions hanging around their necks; close inspection shows that each medallion carries a different miniature portrait of a dog. Other forms of decoration include dots and hearts, often on a clear yellow background, and many examples have glass eyes.

It is interesting to see how later designers have been influenced by these idiosyncratic models. Pairs of stylized "loving cats" so often seen in gift shops in France, have floral decoration on their backs. Many Italian ceramic cats echo the Gallé pose, often with necks elongated to the point of caricature. Cheap little

bone-china cats currently being made in Staffordshire in England to be sold in street markets have the same giraffe-like necks, and their bodies are patterned with bunches of pink roses. Even soft toys were given the Gallé look: in 1912, the ever-enterprising Dean's Rag Book Company made a set of three lucky black cats advertised as *Tiddles and her Two Cheeky Kittens* (two shillings for the whole family), all shaped exactly like Gallé cats. In the 1920s, *Lucky Luke* arrived, described as "a fantastical cat with a long neck, a merry smile, weird spectacles, and a squeaky tail," again very much in the Gallé mold.

Germany exported untold tons of china ornaments in the late 19th and early 20th centuries, most of them cheap enough to have adorned quite modest homes. To judge from surviving pieces, a considerable proportion of this vast output featured cozy house cats: they climb up the sides of antique spill-holders and pitchers, play musical instruments, sit at the base of a crescent moon, or

— 20 —

This cat and kitten group in white bisque porcelain is unmarked, but is typical of models made in Germany and exported widely in the last quarter of the 19th century.

simply look decorative. Many are of unglazed bisque; over the years, they may have lost some of their original color.

Springer and Oppenheimer, of Elbogen, Germany, made small ceramic groups specifically for the British market; they were very popular as prizes and souvenirs at fairgrounds. Now referred to as "fairings" and increasingly fashionable among collectors, some display comic characters in slightly risqué situations, but there are also several charming cat groups: *Five o'clock Tea,* a great favorite and comparatively easy to find, has a quintet of cats around a table; *Who Said Rats?* shows an alert cat sitting up in a canopied bed, while another has a cat on top of a dressing table with ruffled skirts. These groups were made by various firms over several decades, and the modeling varies tremendously; even so, anybody comparing one of the German originals with a modern reproduction could easily see the difference between them. Apart from inferior molding and decoration, the repro-

ductions have a raised bar running across the underside of the base.

Early this century, several English companies made modest little china souvenirs bearing the coats-of-arms of hundreds of British towns and

This amusing early 20th-century ceramic mother-and-kitten group has a receptacle for matches on the side. The matches could be lit by striking them against the mother's back; hence the instruction: "Don't scratch me, scratch Mother."

cities. All sorts of small objects were decorated in this way – miniature vases, holders for hat-pins, tiny Noah's Arks, and thousands of lucky black cats. William Goss was the inventor of this heraldic porcelain, but of all his many designs, only one portrays a cat. It was left to other firms, such as Arcadia, the Willow Art China company, and Grafton, to produce black cats on bicycles, on seesaws, suffering from toothache, and generally performing unlikely feats. Some collectors confine themselves to these heraldic cats and still manage to fill shelf after shelf.

In 1902, after several years of patient research, Royal Doulton produced a magnificent rouge flambé glaze. Doulton's process recreated the superb blood-red and ruby effects achieved by Chinese potters of the Sung dynasty, and a fiery cat with this wonderfully rich decoration would shine in any collection. The first flambé cat dates from 1902, but Doulton introduced a new model in

1977, which is probably easier to find and correspondingly less expensive.

A truly representative collection would call for a cat from Denmark's Royal Copenhagen factory, perhaps one of the firm's lovely Siamese. A Scottish Wemyss cat, fancifully decorated with roses or four-leaved clovers, also deserves a place. It goes without saying that traditional Chinese and Japanese ceramic cats should be included; both countries are still exporting cat figures, and there are plenty to be found at quite modest prices.

The Royal Crown Derby Company is making a series of "Royal Cats," designed by Robert Jefferson. The aim is to produce porcelain cats with regal personalities, creatures of the imagination bedecked in gorgeous robes and crowns. The colors are typically Crown Derby – a rich red and blue, lit with 22-carat gold. Obviously they are not cheap, but nor, for the moment, are they difficult to find. Most stockists of Crown

Three heraldic souvenir cat models, are from the early 20th century. Small china ornaments decorated with the coat-of-arms of a town or city were popular British vacation souvenirs.

Derby display them, and of the six issued so far, the Abyssinian Royal Cat, in authentic headgear, is particularly impressive.

Strikingly original decoration is a hallmark of de Bethel cats, made in Rye, one of England's historic Cinque Ports. Joan and David de Bethel's sitting cats are unique: rotund, smiling creatures radiating contentment and dressed in surreal costume, the earliest mid-20th century specimens were made in papier-mâché, and a particularly stylish male wears a jacket covered with prints of ships. The slightly later ceramic models are much given to ruffled collars and cuffs in the manner of Gallé cats; mine has a blue jacket ornamented with decoupage featuring cat and flower "scraps" and is dated 1991. Smaller versions of de Bethel-type cats were made under licence in Taiwan, 3–4½ inches high; a few years ago, they could be seen in ser-

ried ranks in gift stores at bargain prices. Very similar ones are currently being imported in England through the Global Village enterprise, while more are made in the town of Rye itself by the Cinque Port Pottery. There is no mistaking an original de Bethel cat with its special decoration, and early examples are beginning to attract high prices at auction.

English pottery cats from the Winstanley stable are wonderful value. Winstanley is the professional name of a sculptor whose husband is a potter and whose son helps with the painting, and this family partnership produces a variety of models that are completely true to cat life; at first glance, the larger sizes can easily be mistaken for live pets. Like the Gallé cats, Winstanley's models have glass eyes, as do the rather similar, large, life-like creatures produced in Staffordshire, England, by Just Cats. Mike Hinton is another potter specializing

Three Japanese porcelain "beckoning" cats, traditionally supposed to bring good luck and used by shopkeepers to welcome customers. The left- and right-hand examples date from c.1900; the middle one is from c.1935.

in natural-looking cats, also with rather unnerving glass eyes.

Louis Wain designed some china cats, produced in 1914 by an English firm, Max Emmanuel & Co. Contemporaries described them as "futuristic" and "cubist," and it is difficult

This small seated ceramic cat with glass eyes, made in England by Mike Hinton, was purchased in 1992 and is 4½in high.

A ceramic cat measuring 7½in high, painted and then decorated with decoupage, made by Joan de Bethel, of Rye, England. This model is marked *Joan and David de Bethel, Rye, Sussex, 1991.*

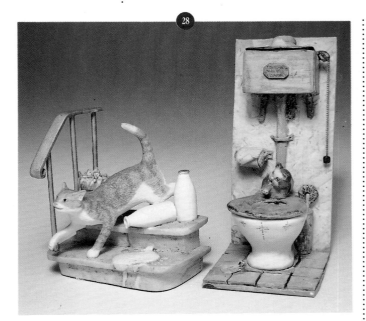

28

These small cat models are cast in modern resins. Such highly detailed figures have become very popular with collectors, and Peter Fagan's *Colour Box* company runs a Collectors' Club in England.

to imagine anything less like the rounded cats in his drawings. Very few survive, partly because World War I broke out shortly after they came onto the market and a consignment on its way to the U.S. was torpedoed. However, it is possible that a keen Wain-collector could find one of these freakish cats, reported to have been modeled in all positions and in all sizes, and with their bodies hollowed out to make holders for flowers.

Louis Wain's biographer, Rodney Dale, mentions seeing just one china figure of a "true" Wain cat which, although signed by the artist, had no maker's or registration mark.

CONTEMPORARY CAT ARTISTS
~

More recently, ceramic cats have been produced by a variety of artists, and most serious collectors will have their favorites – Maisie Seneshall's Siamese, for example, or Agnete Hoy's salt-glaze standing tabby. The Chelsea Pottery wares decorated by Joyce Morgan, a great lover of cats, have rather Louis Wain-like tabbies

in rich browns and yellows; these can be found on tiles, dishes, and pitchers. The Scottish artist Margery Clinton made a model of "Smudge," resident mouser at Glasgow's People's Palace since 1980. Replicas, life-size and in a limited edition of 50, were first sold in 1986, but they were so successful that the artist was commissioned to make a smaller version. Collectors can recognize "Smudge" by his black patches on a predominantly white body and a small black spot on the nose.

American artists who enjoy favor among cat collectors tend to work in more than one medium. Uncle Ted, a.k.a. Thaddeus Krumeich, did ceramic plates and figures as well as lithographs and a series of greeting cards for UNICEF. Mimi Vang Olsen's cats appear on plates, postcards, and books. Lowell Davis, a hot artist of the moment, has designed cat figures, plates, ornaments, and lithographs. Karen Kuykendall is a non-production artist in ceramics, papier mâché, and acrylics whose cats often have an outer space (science fiction) quality.

To meet the demand for miniature furnishings and occupants for dolls' houses, several designers have turned their skills to producing very small ceramic cats. Since dolls' houses now appeal to adults, these scaled-down pieces are intended for collectors and are usually too expensive to be classed as toys, but many of them are very attractive and could be displayed in their own right, without any need for a dolls' house.

There are Wade Pottery figures of both Puss-in-Boots and the Cat-and-Fiddle, and a wide choice of miniature cat models in Peter Fagan's "Colour Box" range. These, like the "Colour Box" teddy bears, are so popular that they have a Collectors' Club, with its own magazine giving news of the latest designs.

CATS AS
TOYS

29

— 29 —

This mechanical cat
with a fan, 6¼in ×
3½in × 2½in, walks
upright on its hind
legs. Made of
lithographed tinplate
between 1890 and
1920, it is possibly
German, but the
maker is unknown.

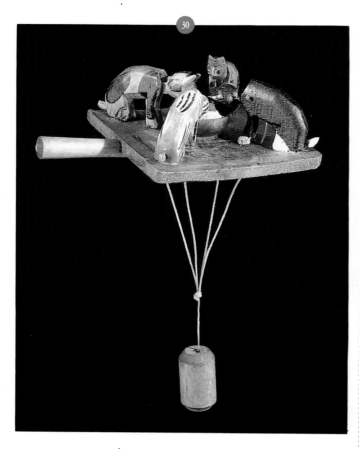

As with ceramic models, collectors looking for nursery cats face strong competition from collectors of antique toys in general. This is now a very popular area, apparently impervious to economic fluctuations, and one in which prices can seem discouragingly high. French and German automata from the Golden Age of toys – say from about 1880 until the outbreak of World War I – are invariably expensive; it would be unrealistic to expect to find a French walking cat by Descamps ("c.1900. covered in white rabbit fur, with green and black glass eyes, pink painted nose, opening mouth . . . lacking whiskers") such as one offered by Sotheby's in 1991 at anything like a bargain price. Even so, huge numbers of mechanical animals were produced at this time; and survivors, often in surprisingly good

working order, do regularly find their way onto the market. It is interesting to compare them with the toys described in old trade catalogs, which include a tantalizing array of cats. In 1912, for example, Sears Roebuck & Co. was advertising walking animals made by Bing, one of Germany's foremost toy manufacturers; a "very realistic" walking cat in silky mohair cloth was recommended as "practically unbreakable and will not easily get out of order" – perhaps there is a faint hint of hope triumphing over experience in the cautious use of "not easily" – while a wind-up cat by the same maker, fully dressed and fitted with roller skates, "moves forward and backward in the most lifelike manner".

Wind-up "clockwork" cats from Japan came later; they are less elaborate, smaller, and geared to the mass market. Examples could still be

found in ordinary toy stores in the 1960s: one was cleverly constructed to toss a ball into the air, another to snatch at a butterfly, and both were packed in pictorial cardboard boxes. Any toy in its original box has an added interest as well as an added value, and this packaging should be preserved. A box holding a wind-up tinplate cat gives the maker's name – Kohler – and the information that it was made in the U.S. zone of Germany, giving a fair indication of its date. Tinplate models from these recent times have become collectible, because legislation on safety means that many are no longer manufactured. Reports of small retailers with "old stock" should be investigated.

In America Fisher-Price Toys, Inc., of East Aurora, New York, produced a number of cat toys including Pop-Up Kritter #455 Tailspin Tabby (1939–43) with leather-type ears, painted face, red paddle, and white feet and tail, #600 Tailspin Tabby Pop-Up (1947), a cat whose motion was controlled by a disk on the bottom of a box, could move in different directions and even collapse, re-styled in 1948 as #610 and made for two years, and #499 Kitty Bell (1950), a pull toy. Tailspin Tabby closely resembles Felix the Cat and is often offered for sale as a Felix the Cat collectible. Sullivan never licensed Fisher-Price to make a Felix toy. Do not be fooled.

— 32 —

This delightful American wooden rocker is known as "Bobbie the rocking pussy cat," and measures 17in × 13½in.

— 33 —

This wooden car, c.1969, with its black kitten chauffeur and five clothed kitten passengers was made in West Germany and purchased in the U.S.

Other American cat toys include: a wooden child's rocker entitled "Bobbie the rocking pussy cat"; Arrow Toys' Kitty (c. 1960), a molded vinyl cat with a turning head and squeaker; Mattel's Cat in the Hat talking doll (1970) that is 11″ high and says "Does your mother know I'm here?"; Playskool's Dog and Cat in a Barrel (1976); and, Chasley's Catsup! (1986), a cat juggling game. A marvelous collection can be assembled of celluloid cats sold in five and ten cent stores during the 1920s through the 1950s. Pay a premium for American-made examples.

A quite different type of toy cat was developed in the United States in the early 1890s, when the Arnold Print Works of North Adams, Massachusetts, patented a design for a mother tabby and two kittens printed on a sheet of cotton fabric. The customer had only to sew together the

two halves – the front and back view of the sitting cat – around an oval base section and then add suitable stuffing. These simple models were surprisingly lifelike; and for almost a hundred years, the basic pattern has been constantly adapted (and, indeed, faithfully reproduced) by other makers. Sears Roebuck's 1912 catalog illustrates a Pussy Meow and Little Dog Tray printed side by side on good quality muslin, with the pair priced at 15 cents. In England, Dean's Rag Book Company included rotund figures of a striped tabby and a mottled ginger, known as Fluffikits, in their catalog of 1920. More recently, Pollocks Toy Museum in London introduced William Henry, a substantial creature some 15 inches high, designed by Maria Wood. Painted velvet cats created by an unnamed English artist in the 1960s and sold through interior decorators also followed the basic design.

Soft stuffed toys representing cats come in all sorts, shapes, and sizes. Early models can sometimes be identified from old advertisements and trade catalogs, while others like Steiff and Dean's often retain their ear-buttons or sewn-on labels. As for present-day examples, a survey of a few large toy departments will show how impossible it would be to list all the excellent cats being produced, and collectors must make their own personal choices. For myself, I still regret not buying a tabby mother complete with a family of sucking kittens that could be attached to her by their ingenious "velcro" mouths. In addition to cats from toy-making firms, there are some lovely, highly individual models made by artists working independently; Sylvia King, for example, who used to design for Dean's, now makes beautiful, natural-looking animals, including cats and kittens, to order.

— 34 —

A stuffed cotton cloth cat, known as a Fluffikit, was made in England by Dean's Rag Book Co. Ltd. around 1925. The kit could also be bought as a length of fabric to be sewn together at home. Its height is 7in.

STEIFF CATS

~

Every collection ought to have at least one Steiff cat, and fortunately there is no shortage, as the famous German firm is still producing a wide variety of beautiful stuffed toys. Their vintage cats, however, dating from the early 1900s, do have a rarity value; auction prices for these are correspondingly high. Their Puss-in-Boots cats, made about 1910, had a teddy bear-type body with jointed arms and legs, but most Steiff cats look natural, whether lying, sitting, or standing.
Steiff claims that all its toys carry the well-known trademark metal button in the left ear. This certainly applies to sets of Steiff dog and elephant ninepins in my collection; the cat ninepins seem to have been made in exactly the same way, from rigidly-stuffed felt on turned wooden bases, but they are without the ear buttons, so no one can be absolutely certain. Whatever their provenance, though, the eight gray kittens accompanied by a white "king" in a scarlet coat and crown have great charm. Like all felt toys, they need to be protected from moths; make regular inspections, as moths are fast workers.

— 35 —

This stuffed cat toy, c.1920–30, made by the famous German firm of Steiff (better known for its teddy bears) is complete with the manufacturer's button in its left ear.

— 36 —

A set of cat ninepins, made from felt, are stuffed and mounted on turned wooden bases. They lack the famous "button in the ear" identification, but it seems likely that they were made in Germany by Steiff, c.1900.

PAPER CATS

~

Tremendous advances in color-printing techniques in the late 19th century had far-reaching effects on toy production. A combination of embossing and chromolithography produced brilliant paper "scraps" and cutout figures, while jigsaw puzzles, board games, building blocks, and elaborate picture books all depended on color printing for their impact. One of the most important publishers, especially for cat-lovers, was the firm of Raphael Tuck. Tuck himself went to England from Germany in 1865 and immediately made a success of his small business selling and framing pictures. By 1870 he was producing chromolithographs and oleographs, and in 1871 he published his first Christmas card. The whole family worked together, and in 1881, by which time a flourishing export business had been built up, the firm became Raphael Tuck & Sons. During the 1890s and early 1900s, they produced a huge variety of paper-based novelties, often taking the trouble to patent their ingenious designs in England, France,

Germany, and the U.S. Fortunately, these official patent documents are preserved, but all the firm's own records were lost in an air raid on London during World War II. This makes any collection of Raphael Tuck cats all the more important from a research point of view, as it is only by collectors sharing information that the history of these most attractive paper toys can be pieced together. Barbara Whitton Jendrick has done an immense amount of work on the whole of the company's vast output, and collectors should refer to her book, *Paper Dolls and Paper Toys of Raphael Tuck & Sons* (1971).

Tuck's cats appear on a great variety of embossed "scraps," used for sticking in albums or decorating children's walls; a set of nine large "scrap" cats in the *Gigantic Relief* series has a label announcing that the firm, now a limited company, was "by Special Appointment Publishers to her Majesty the Queen." Since Queen Victoria died in 1901, and Raphael Tuck became a limited company in the same year, these particular cats can be dated exactly. Between 1901 and 1910, the com-

— 37 —

These *Cat Show* paper scraps from a folding, panoramic screen are by Perry and Co. Limited of London and also by Raphael Tuck of London, printed in Bavaria, probably c.1900–1910.

38

pany was described as "Publishers to Their Majesties the King and Queen and T.R.H. the Prince and Princess of Wales" (i.e. Edward VII, Queen Alexandra, and the future George V and Queen Mary). This announcement appears on the back of a cardboard cat with movable head and legs that enable it to adopt various poses. Information about the cat family is also printed on the back – its Latin name, the characteristics of different breeds, and the fact that "cats are usually kept to destroy mice." Another cat of this Edwardian era was included in a boxed set of *Father Tuck's Marionettes:* this one is a humanized mother tabby wearing a skirt and blouse and carrying three kittens in her string-operated arms. A magnificently dressed Puss-in-Boots has the same string-operated mechanism.

Cats with a rocking movement were another Tuck favorite; the first seem to have been part of a boxed set of six *Rocking Horses* dating from the 1890s. One horse has a cat riding on its back with three kittens in a basket on the rocker, while another has a dog rider with a cat clinging to

— 38 —

This cat is one of the many paper and cardboard novelties produced by Raphael Tuck and Sons. Dating from 1901 to 1910, this model has a movable head and legs, and educational material about the cat family is printed on the back.

its shoulders. These were followed about a decade later by *Father Tuck's Toy Rockers,* made up of "10 mechanical models with novel movement of happy children, comic animals, etc., etc." and including another dressed-up tabby.

Another set of rockers was described on the box as "realistic models of domestic and wild animals ... hours of endless delight"; this time, the cat is again a natural-looking animal on all fours, standing on a bright Turkish carpet of a type so evocative of the period. Some of the animals from this set, including the cat and a St. Bernard, have been reproduced in England by Mamelok.

J.W. Spear & Sons manufactured a string-operated cardboard toy called *Snowball,* as part of its Jolly Jumpers series. This "very solidly made ... most durable toy" is illustrated in the company's 1910 catalog. Sad to say, I have been unable to find a *Snowball* myself but other collectors could well be luckier.

BOARD, CARD, AND SKILL GAMES
~

Games with a cat cover or theme are extremely popular among collectors. *Kat En Muis,* a Dutch lithograph printed paper game from the late nineteenth century, features drawings by American illustrator Palmer Cox. *Miaou Miaou!,* a Snake and Ladder variation featuring cats going up or coming down with seeming disregard for good or bad behavior, was manufactured by an anonymous French publisher about 1905. Many games, such as Parker Brothers *The Black Cat Fortune Telling Game,* remained in production for decades,

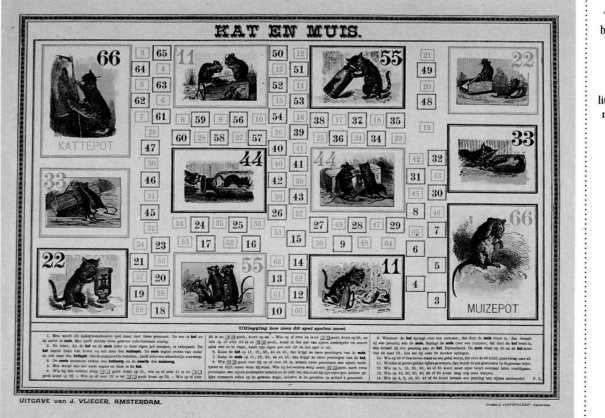

This highly amusing board game of *Kat en Muis* is made by J. Vlieger from Amsterdam and printed on lithographed paper. It measures 22½in × 17½in.

their appeal kept current through cover redesign.

J.W. Spear & Sons, another Anglo-German firm, active throughout the twentieth century, produced a number of games with a cat theme. Collectors eagerly seek copies of *Pussy Ball Game* (about 1905), *Little Kittens Tidley Wink Game* (about 1910), and *The Cats' Mansion* (mid-1980s), a complicated board game with model cats for counters. By good fortune I was able to acquire this game, which is already hard to find. A fellow-collector, having searched long and unsuccessfully, finally discovered a shop with several boxes still in stock. Sensibly she bought them all and generously offered them to friends – a splendid example of the wisdom of snapping up attractive items that can all too quickly go out of circulation.

However, the premier cat games originated in America. The high

— 40 —

The Black Cat Fortune Telling Game, issued by Parker Brothers in 1897, is described as a game "for all seasons but highly recommended for Halloween."

41

— **41** —

The Three Little Kittens board game was produced by the American firm of Milton Bradley Co. The box is shown here with dimensions of 7½in × 7½in × ½in. The box has the game printed on the bottom of it and also contains a spinner.

quality lithography covers of McLoughlin Brothers bookcase game *Games of Cats and Mice-Gantlope and Lost Diamond* (c. 1900), *Combination Tiddley Winks, Game of Catching Mice* (1888), *Game of Snap* (1902), and *Pussy Cat Ten Pins* (c. 1900) are a positive delight. Milton Bradley manufactured the *Game of Puss: Would Make A Cat Laugh* (c. 1910), *Game of Puss in Boots* (1908), *Hickery Dickery Dock* (c. 1900), *Pussy Ring Game* (early 1900s), and *The Three Little Kittens* (c. 1910). The lid of Parker Brothers *The Amusing Game of Kilkenny Cats* (c. 1890s) features dueling cats derived from an Old English ballad. Rosebud Art Company's *Kitty Kat Kup Ball* was a popular 1930s game.

Board, card, and skill games are collected primarily for their cover art. While it would be a joy to find any of these old cat games to buy, enthusiasts will find many of their playing surfaces reproduced in Erika Bruce's *The Great Cat Game Book* (London: Michael Joseph, 1985), based on games in the collections of Erika Bruce and Ellery Yale Wood

along with examples from the Washington Dolls' House and Toy Museum. The pages can be detached and actually used for play. Be sensible and buy two copies – one to play with and one to keep intact.

Like many game manufacturers, Parker Brothers recycled their art by using it for other toy products in their line. The art for Parker Brothers *Old Maid* board game is identical to that found on the *Comic Animal Picture Puzzle* jigsaw puzzle set.

Over the years, various companies have made attempts to give toy cats convincing voices. German toymakers in the 19th century used a bellows mechanism, with the cat toy attached to the upper part; when the cat was pressed down, it caused the bellows to emit a meow sound. Bellows toys were also made in 19th-century America, where they were known as pipsqueaks or squeak toys; many originated in Pennsylvania, made from wood, papier-mâché, or plaster of Paris. The Henry Ford Museum has several interesting examples of pipsqueak cats, one of them with a mouse in its mouth and

— **42** —

This cat squeak toy is probably of German origin, c. 1850–1870. The squeak is heard by depressing the cat into the base. It measures approximately 2in square.

42

JIGSAW PUZZLES
~

Jigsaw puzzles offer another excellent opportunity to build a specialized cat collection. Three jigsaw puzzles that would enhance any collection are: (1) J. W. Barfoot's Miss Tabby's Party *(c. 1860), featuring a hand-colored lithograph showing cats at a tea party with four smaller pictures entitled "Going to the Party," "Arrival at the Party," "The Ball," and "Return from the Party"; (2) Milton Bradley's* Pussy Cat Puzzle Box *(c. 1900) touting a lithograph cover of a bevy of cats skating on an ice-covered pond along with three puzzles — cats attending a fancy banquet dinner, kittens playing after school, and the ice-skating cats shown on the cover; and, (3) Parker Brothers* Robber Kitten Picture Puzzle Set *(c. 1920s), two puzzles — one showing a cat robbing a stagecoach and the other a domestic scene with a young kitten chasing a mouse up a clock.*

— **43** —

Miss Tabby's Party, by J. W. Barfoot would enhance any collection with a hand-colored lithograph and original packaging.

— **44** —

This puzzle, c.1920s, represents the second part of *The Robber Kitten* by Parker Brothers.

When looking for cat jigsaw puzzles, make certain to check children's puzzle sets. Cat motifs are a popular theme for children's puzzles. Artwork by well-known illustrators of children's books often is spun-off as jigsaw puzzles. In an unusual instance C. M. Burd's illustration for the children's poem "Little Tommy Tucker" was used as an advertising jigsaw puzzle premium for Famous Biscuits. Finally, do not overlook the contemporary cat puzzle toys of the modern "arts and crafts" movement. Examples from a company called Monkey Puzzle are especially desirable. Richard Rothbard of Sugarloaf, New York, manufactures a "Desk Catty," a three dimensional cat jigsaw puzzle with holes for paper clips, pencils, and stamps. The list goes on and on.

45

45

Four glass slides for a Victorian "magic lantern," c.1910. These comic cats would have been shown during the intermission between the main presentations of a slide show before the days of motion pictures.

another, rarer, model of a cat lying down beside a kitten.

Only recently have collectors begun to appreciate the charm and interest of cats on old magic-lantern slides, and their decorative potential. Until well into this century, magic-lantern shows were a popular form of entertainment for all ages, and millions of mass-produced slides – religious, educational, and amusing – were produced. Most of the cat slides, usually sold in boxes of eight, were aimed at juvenile audiences and included the complete history of Dick Whittington and His Cat – in twelve scenes – and nursery rhyme characters such as the Cat and the Fiddle. Puss-in-Boots was another favorite set. One of the biggest manufacturers was Butcher and Son

of London, trading under the name of Primus; boxes of Primus slides (costing about two shillings before World War I) can still be found at quite reasonable prices in antique stores and collectors' fairs.

In 1907 London's Army and Navy Stores' catalog listed a tempting assortment of magic-lantern slides, with some single "motto" slides designed to punctuate the main attractions. Thus a performance could be introduced with a Christmas greeting, described as "very funny and seasonable, two cats in a hamper with their heads over the side." A "Hush" motto was ornamented with a monkey feeding a cat, and when the lantern got overheated, or the audience too excited, "An Interval" could be announced by either "Cats

Nursing Kittens" or "A Kitten Pie."

Toymakers in the Far East are producing all kinds of cats, many of them obviously designed for the Western market. During the 1980s, some attractive soft-bodied cat-dolls, with ceramic heads and limbs and dressed in old-fashioned cotton dolls' clothes, arrived from Taiwan. The same type of round-faced Victorian-looking cats are to be found among the miniature animals in the *Sylvanian Families* series; there are five members of the cat household, and here again collectors would do well to buy them on sight.

— 46 —

These cat dolls were made by Tracey Gallup of Royal Oak, Michigan. The gray male and white female, dated c.1978, have human hands and slippered feet, while the beige child-cat, signed and dated 1981, has four paws plus a grinning mask and a lucky fish.

— 47 —

This cloth toy cat from China, made of pink cotton with painted spots and glass eyes, was bought in the 1960s. It measures 7¾in.

(48)

— (48) —

This magnificent pair of brass candlesticks was made in Austria in about 1885 for the French market. One cat is based on Dore's illustrations for Perrault's *Puss-in-Boots*, while the other represents Madame D'Aulnoy's *White Cat* in 17th-century dress.

ILLUSTRATED BOOKS
~

Probably the most famous of all cat illustrations is Gustave Doré's magnificent *Puss-in-Boots* from *Perrault, Contes,* published in France in 1861. This is no cozy fireside pet, but a menacing creature with sharp claws and dead mice hanging from his leather belt; the engraving, constantly reproduced in books about children's literature, shows Puss in 17th-century costume as befits a character whose adventures were first published in 1697. This dashing *chevalier* was turned into a three-dimensional model and was, in a slightly different pose, transformed into a statue, by the French sculptor Gabriel Edouard Baptiste Pech (1854–1930), that forms part of the monument to Charles Perrault in Paris.

Illustrations of such literary cats as Puss-in-Boots would make a most interesting collection, representing the work of Doré, Cruikshank, Walter Crane, Kate Greenaway, and other popular artists. *The White Cat, Dick Whittington,* and *Dame Wiggins of Lee and Her Seven Wonderful Cats* are just three stories of cats that have gone through countless editions and inspired many illustrators.

Nineteenth-century books in fine bindings include several volumes devoted to cats: both *Stories about Cats* by Mrs. Surr (1882) and *Tales from Catland by an Old Tabby* (c.1877) also have illustrations by Harrison Weir, which makes them doubly attractive. Harrison Weir loved cats and drew them beautifully, and any book with his illustrations, no matter how battered, deserves careful consideration. The same of course applies to the innumerable books with illustrations of Louis Wain; often these volumes have suffered damage from being childhood favorites, and so have lost their appeal to serious book collectors, but the true cat-lover will still find them irresistible.

The Anglo-German firm of Ernest Nister published a stream of lavishly illustrated nursery books in the 1890s and early 1900s, many of them with pictures that popped up when the pages were turned, or which could be revolved to show a completely different scene. Stories about small domestic animals were often mere pegs on which to hang full-page color pictures of kittens or puppies provided by artists of the caliber of Louis Wain, G. H. Thompson, William Foster, and Helena Maguire (see page 73). Usually the illustrations were printed in Bavaria; Nister handled publication in London, while the New York side of the business was in the hands of E. P. Dutton & Co. *Fun and Frolic, The Playtime Book, Four-footed Friends,* and *Very*

49

— 49 —

Two highly collectible cat picture books: *The Playtime Book,* published by Ernest Nister, was illustrated by Helena Maguire (early 20th century); *With Louis Wain in Pussyland* was published by Raphael Tuck around 1910–20.

— 50 —

These models of Beatrix Potter's *Ribby* and *Miss Moppett* are made in bone china by Beswick of England. Several manufacturers now produce Beatrix Potter figures, giving collectors a wide choice. Their measurements are 3½in and 3in high.

Funny are typical Nister titles, all full of delightful cats.

Like Louis Wain, Beatrix Potter occupies a special place in the world of cat-collecting, thanks to her immortal characters Tom Kitten, Miss Moppet, Ribby, and Simpkin. Besides the well-loved books, collectors could look out for ceramic models, toys, and printed textiles featuring these cats. Tom Kitten and his sisters also appeared with other Beatrix Potter animals on a wallpaper frieze first published in Britain and the United States in 1952.

Kathleen Hale's *Orlando: the Marmalade Cat* is another favorite, first appearing in the 1940s. Garth Williams, Barbara Cooney, Wanda Gag, and Ronald Searle are all well known for their cat illustrations; Graham Oakley's *Church Cat,* Nicola Bayley's *The Patchwork Cat* and Judith Kerr's *Mog* rub shoulders with the felines of Martin Leman,

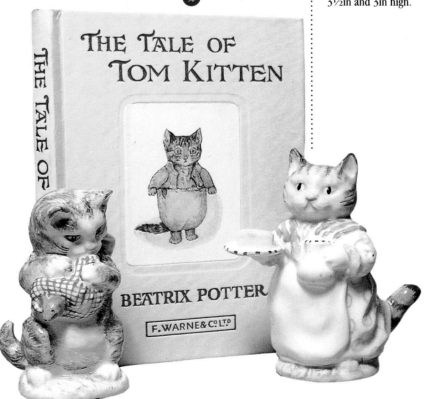

50

51

A stuffed, plushy Cat in the Hat doll, holding a *Cat in the Hat* book autographed by its author, Dr. Seuss. The main character of the book inspired the toy which was made in 1983 by Coleco and stands 25in tall.

Robert Goldstrom, and Zoe Stokes. So many striking picture books have been published in recent years that most collectors are forced through lack of space to be selective, though this can involve some very difficult choices.

In America the most famous literary cat is The Cat in the Hat, a creature created by Ted Geisel, known by his more common monicker – Dr. Seuss. Random House published the first edition of *The Cat in the Hat* in 1957. The book was so successful that Random House created a separate division, Beginner Books, for Geisel. The Cat in the Hat bibliography includes: *The Cat in the Hat Comes Back* (1958), *The Cat in the Hat Song Book* (1967), *The Cat's Quizzer* (1976), and *I Can Read with My Eyes Shut!* (1978). Dr. Seuss items are one of the hottest segments of the American collectibles market with The Cat in the Hat objects leading the pack.

No short list of American children's books about cats can reflect the enormous variety of titles that are available. The following are merely a starting point to discover the richness of this collectible field: Esther Averill's Jenny the Black cat series published by Harper & Row; Margaret Wise Brown's *Sneakers, Pussy Willow,* and *Where Have You Been,* published by Simon & Schuster; Mary Calhoun's *Nine Lives of Homer C. Cat* and *The Witch of Hissing Hill* published by Morrow; and, Frances Louise Davis and Richard Lockridge's *The Nameless Cat, The Lucky Cat,* and *The Proud Cat* published by Lippencott.

Almost all of America's leading children's illustrators tackled a cat story at one time or another. The art of C. M. Burd and Fern Bisel Peat appears in the books and jigsaw puzzles of Saalfield Publishing while

Ruth E. Newton's drawings grace the books and jigsaw puzzles of Whitman Publishing. Every major American children's book publisher tackled the traditional, generic cat story, e.g., Three White Kittens, Puss-in-Boots, etc. Among the finest are the books of McLoughlin Brothers with their high quality lithography.

Another excellent source for cat illustrations by famous as well as lesser known artists are covers of juvenile and specialized magazines. When Herman D. Umbstaetter launched *The Black Cat* magazine in 1895, he was gambling that Americans would buy a monthly devoted to short fiction by amateur writers. By the third year, monthly circulation exceeded 200,000. For the first several years, every cover featured a

— 52 —

The White Kitten, a children's story book of 12 pages, measures 3in × 5in, and was published by Valentine & Sons, Dundee, London, and Montreal.

This puzzle set by Saalfield Publishing Co., No. 567, is called *Kitty-Cat Picture Puzzle Box*. It measures 8¾in × 10¾in and contains six jigsaws by the highly acclaimed artist Fern Bisel Peat.

black cat in scenes ranging from a bicycle rider to a court jester, the work of Nelly Littlehal Umbstaetter, the publisher's wife. Black cats were featured in the decorative motif throughout the magazine, usually entwined with the first letter of the first work of each story. The magazine ceased publication in 1923. No collection is complete without several issues of *The Black Cat*.

CHILDREN'S CHINA
~

Ceramics for children fall into two groups, both of interest to cat collectors. First, there are miniature tea and dinner services for dolls, made in great profusion during the 19th and early 20th centuries; then there are the plates, mugs, and bowls made for children to use themselves.

Most of the earliest toy services are from Staffordshire, although they were also produced by other British potteries. Later on, European and Japanese firms exported vast quantities of dolls' tableware, usually made in cheap porcelain.

English examples of the period c.1820–1880 are avidly sought by serious collectors in this highly specialized field. Ideally, however, they are looking for complete sets, sometimes up to seventy pieces, in perfect condition, while the dedicated cat-enthusiast will be delighted to find a single item, even a damaged one, if it has a feline decoration. Cats were apparently not popular with the

— 54 —

This English toy cup and saucer featuring cats and other animals was made by Copeland in 1860.

three remarkable new developments: an increase in the number of illustrated books, the use of cheap transfer-printing on earthenware, and a general softening in parents' attitude toward their children, all of which resulted, along with much else, in the manufacture of these charming pieces. Many had religious or educational overtones, and "alphabet" plates are quite common, often incorporating the obvious "C for CAT" mnemonic. Popular engravings and book illustrations were used as a basis for most of the decorations. *Dame Trot and her Cat* appears on a plate from the Cobridge Staffordshire factory of J. & R. Clews (1818–35), the print taken from a children's book published in 1820. A *Hey-Diddle-Diddle* cat decorates another plate of the same period; yet another has the beautiful cat and kittens engraving taken from Gottfried Mind's painting. There are, too, plates and mugs decorated with a single cat figure, one of the most appealing a plump striped animal captioned "TABBY." Others to look out for are *The Cats' Concert* (a group of ten cats singing, with the

manufacturers of the very early services, probably because they aimed to reproduce toy versions of the real dinner services of the period; decorated with classical and romantic landscapes, these were more suitable as backgrounds for goats, dogs, ponies, and peacocks than for frolicsome cats. However, in 1860, the Copeland factory made a miniature tea service printed with various animals including a cat, and in 1888 a *Nursery Rhymes* design was registered by the Hanley Staffordshire firm of Whittaker & Co. which has plates decorated with Cat-and-Fiddle groups. Some years ago, I was pleased to find a toy teapot, probably German and dating from about 1900, with a beribboned tabby printed on the side. By this time, cats were well-established subjects for decorations on toy tea services, and collectors will find a wide choice. An out-of-the-ordinary service, c.1930, is composed of pieces made in the shape of cats, colored pink.

Unlike these scaled-down services for dolls, plates and mugs for children's own use were decorated with cats from the beginning. The early 19th century saw the combination of

— 55 —

Two child's plates. The one on the left, bought in the 1960s but inspired by a much earlier design, was made in England by Adams by Staffordshire. The same cats in a basket were used in a 19th-century American advertisement. The right-hand plate comes from a 1920s tea set called the "Wireless Set," made by Heathcote China.

56

A child's earthenware plate with a molded floral border is decorated with a transfer print of a young girl holding a swaddled cat. Entitled *The Young Nurse*, it is English and dates from 1830–1840.

words "music hath charms to sooth (sic) the savage breast") *The Young Nurse* (a child holding a wrapped-up cat), *Little Titty* (girl standing, holding a kitten), and a cat with its paw in a goldfish bowl.

Later pieces were decorated with Louis Wain cats: I have one of the heavy-rimmed "Baby's Plate" kind, printed with *The Puppy's Punishment,* showing a puppy being forced to take medicine by a matronly cat while two kittens watch, and a mug with a scene of kittens taking a bath. They are unmarked, but must belong to the early years of this century.

In the 1960s, the long-established English firm of Adams produced children's plates with a printed alphabet border and a central print of two cats in a shopping basket captioned *In a Soft Place;* completely in the style of the previous century, the print is almost identical with lithographs supplied by J. H. Bufford's Sons, of Boston, Massachusetts, to New England manufacturers as an advertising give-away piece in the mid-to-late 1800s. Among those who made use of these cats was Charles H. Richardson, a maker of cough-drops and later a candy manufacturer and grocer.

57

A child's mug decorated with a Louis Wain illustration of "The Cat's Bathtime." Beside it stands a modern Louis Wain reproduction used as a greeting card. The mug is unmarked, but is English and dates from the early 20th century.

CHAPTER THREE

CATS
AT
CHRISTMAS
AND OTHER FESTIVALS

58

— 58 —

Pat Albeck is the
designer of this tin
showing a tabby cat
under a bunch of
mistletoe. The
provenance is
unfortunately not
known.

By the 1880s, Christmas card manufacturers had realized that cats spelled success; no other animal had quite the same gift for conveying a cheery greeting, whether portrayed simply sitting beside a cozy fire, mixing a plum pudding, or throwing snowballs. The range of cards available during the last two decades of the 19th century offered an enormous choice and, since they were bought in huge numbers and often carefully preserved afterward, an astonishing variety has survived to delight today's collectors.

Raphael Tuck, Marcus Ward, and Hildesheimer and Faulker were the leading London firms producing Christmas cards at this period, while L. Prang and Company led the field in the U.S. Among the many Prang cards featuring cats is one with a tabby playing a cello to a little dog, with the typically punning quatrain:

> The "mews"ic moves
> without a "paws"
> In quite "dog"matic measure,
> I only add a friendly "claws":
> "May this card bring you pleasure"

Although most English cards were actually printed in Germany by means of very sophisticated chromolithographic techniques, the designs were by British artists and relied on unmistakably British roly-poly cats quite unlike the thin, cross-looking felines of continental illustrators. Helena Maguire was a prolific designer of greeting cards, and her delightful cats take part in all sorts of seasonal activities; although they never wear clothes, apart from neck ribbons, her cats can stand upright on their hind legs, carry shopping baskets, and use their forepaws like hands. In one especially charming study, three cats are grouped around a table eating plum pudding; a small Austrian bronze model is of an identical group, and it is clear that it was copied from the Christmas card design. It would be interesting to know if other collectors have noticed examples of this particular type of cross-fertilization.

Helena Maguire's work is often signed either in full or with her initials, but as Hildesheimer and Faulkner seldom included the artist's name on their products, it is impossible to be sure which of their many cat cards

An amusing double-sided Christmas card shows kittens breaking into a toy drum. Published by Hildesheimer & Faulkner of London, it was printed in Germany, c.1880–90.

she designed. This firm published a series of very attractive double-sided cards with Maguire-type cats, cleverly combining both front and back views of some little tableau, such as a group of cats climbing out of a barrel, or a family of kittens breaking into a toy drum.

By the turn of the century, Yuletide cats were everywhere. Frances Simpson, author of *A Book of Cats* (1902), wrote that "the most casual observer cannot have failed to remark the wonderful development in late years of Catty Christmas souvenirs . . . we have cat almanacks, cat calendars and cat annuals, and I can testify to the innumerable Christmas cards with designs of all sorts and conditions which have found their way into my hands." By this time, of course, Louis Wain's famous comic cats had burst upon the scene, enlivening not only cards, but a whole succession of Christmas numbers of popular magazines as well. Louis Wain's seasonal set pieces like *A Cats' Christmas Dance* (containing over a hundred and twenty cats and kittens) or *The Merry-Go-Round* (cats and dogs on a carousel) were eagerly collected, and a contemporary writer has left a touching account of some wretchedly poor children pausing in front of a barber's window where one of his drawings was displayed: "Hunger, cold and misery were all dispelled," it was reported, as the children laughed at the antics of Wain's favorite cat Peter "in frolicsome mood" entertaining at a large cats' tea party.

Although many of Louis Wain's large drawings were published by *The Illustrated London News,* he also worked for other magazines, and it is worthwhile looking through issues of the 1880s and '90s in case they contain any of his cats. A page of some of the cats seen at the Crystal Palace Cat Show appeared in 1887, while

60

Professor Frederick's Performing Cats, then on the London stage, were featured in time for Christmas the following year. These are both in *The Illustrated London News,* but The *Merry-go-Round* appeared in *The Lady's Pictorial* (1888) and in 1896 *The Penny Illustrated Paper* gave away "two of the funniest Christmas plates ever published," also of course by Louis Wain.

Fortunately, a great number of early cards were pasted into albums, and although it is a pity to see a beautiful old album broken up and its contents dispersed, there are some which have disintegrated to the point where a dealer is probably justified in offering individual items. Louis Wain cards are never cheap, but a small amount could secure a good cat Christmas card by another artist

— **60** —

A cutout Christmas card, c.1900, shows a kitten in a baby's crib. It has been pasted with many others in a scrapbook.

delicacy of chromolithography; an assortment of late 20th-century cards by Anne Robinson, Ditz, Lesley Anne Ivory, and Martin Leman – to name only a few – showing modern designs allied to present-day printing techniques, would, however, make a really interesting addition to a serious collection.

One of 1991's most striking cards shows two of Mimi Vang Olsen's wide-eyed cats lying under a Christmas tree, its branches hung with cat-shaped ornaments. In real life, inquisitive pets would quickly have detached all the decorations, but if a safe place can be found, cat-lovers can have a tree absolutely weighed down with all the cat ornaments now being made. The majority come from Taiwan, but the designs are obviously European or American. There are simple jointed wooden figures like miniature jumping-jacks, natural-looking cats in baskets, and more elaborate, rounded, wooden cat-dolls in brightly painted clothes, all with cords for hanging.

— 61 —

This large striking, Christmas card showing a tree hung with cats, is by Mimi Vang Olsen.

of the 1880s or '90s. Specialist dealers come and go, but they tend to congregate in areas like Cecil Court, just north of London's Trafalgar Square. Others are to be found in antiques centers up and down the British Isles, and at regular ephemera and postcard fairs. Anyone wanting to concentrate on this aspect of cat-collecting would do well to join the Ephemera Society, situated in Fitzroy Square, central London.

Today's card manufacturers, recognizing a line that sells well, have revived many of the early designs, including several Louis Wains and even more of the anonymous Maguire-type Victorian cats. Welcome as these are, comparison with the originals shows that modern photographic techniques still cannot recapture the

— 62 —

Two glass Christmas tree ball decorations. The one showing two kittens in a basket is from the 1930s; the lone silver cat is more recent, dating from the 1980s.

Christmas cat
decorations; (left) a
three-dimensional cat
face, made in the
1980s in Taiwan;
(right) black cat
design by Lesley
Holmes – made in
1991 in Taiwan;
(front) a small seated
Chinese cat made of
frosted "glass" dates
from the 1980s.

ORNAMENTS
~

In the late 1980s, some small ornaments representing long-haired cats
arrived from China, looking like
opaque glass, but in fact made from
lightweight plastic. They were incre-
dibly cheap and, needless to say, are
no longer to be found – yet another
case of an "unconsidered trifle"
becoming a collectors' item almost
overnight. Well-made metal "flats"
based on Martin Leman's cats are
currently being made in Taiwan.
Elegantly packed, they sell in the
quality market and are certainly worth
a place in a collection of modern
Christmas-tree cats.

Old tree ornaments featuring cats
are scarce, but given the fragility of
all glass balls, it seems miraculous

that any have survived, let alone the
few cats among them. In the U.S.,
however, there are enthusiasts who
have built up amazing collections of
vintage ornaments, including not only
those made of glass, but others made
of cotton, wood, metal, straw, and
wax. Robert Brenner, who has done
painstaking research into the subject,
shows several German glass cats in
his book *Christmas Past* (Schiffer,
1985), including a rare clip-on
ornament portraying both the fiddle-
playing cat and the laughing dog,
and I have two hanging decorations,
probably from the 1930s.

Miniature Christmas-tree lights also
come in cat shapes: Germany, Austria,
and Hungary were exporting fancy
electric lights as early as 1908, including a Puss-in-Boots figure. The

Four miniature ornaments in bisque porcelain are intended to be used as cake decorations. The smaller black cats in the foreground are trinkets found in Christmas "crackers." All are German, c.1920–30.

Eveready Company of America soon followed with similar lights, but once Japanese manufacturers had got into their stride, they virtually dominated the market because of their low production costs. Until World War II, Japanese companies exported hundreds of different models, many of them based on nursery rhyme and fairy-tale characters and aimed at European and American buyers; a determined collector might be rewarded with one of the fairy-tale cats.

Miniature unglazed porcelain figures for decorating Christmas cakes are popular collectors' items. Most belong to the 1920s and '30s and were made in Germany, and the majority are the familiar snow-baby children. There are, though, several Christmas cats among these small treasures, as well as some cat candle-holders for birthday cakes.

Even smaller cats with Christmas associations are found in Christmas crackers of the early 20th century; these are tiny black glass cats in a sitting position, almost certainly made in Bohemia. Some elaborate ones have diamond-bright eyes and wear a narrow metal collar with a bead attached. It seems astonishing now that so much care should have been lavished on minute objects intended to give such transitory pleasure, but apparently many of the trinkets in early crackers were suitable for dolls' houses, and some of the black cats found permanent homes there.

Sets of plum-pudding charms, including silver cats and other good luck emblems, used to be sold everywhere and renewed every year. Now they too are difficult to find, and any collector interested in either cats or Christmas memorabilia should snap up these modest little charms before they disappear completely.

Since December is the time for buying new calendars and diaries, they could be considered as related to Christmas. There is always a choice assortment of cat calendars – sentimental, comic, and artistic, and some

BLACK CATS
~

Halloween brings the cat to the fore, especially the black cat. The origins of Halloween trace back to the Celtic festival of Samhaim, when ghosts, witches, and demons roamed the earth in search of peace. The cat's link with witchcraft, resulting in tales and superstitions that linger to the present, made it part of Halloween lore.

Irish and Scottish immigrants brought the tradition for mischief, noisemaking, and trickery on October 31, All Hallows Eve, to the U.S. The golden age of American Halloween collectibles dates from the 1920s through the 1950s. During this era the Halloween cat was portrayed as a sinister creature with hunched back and bushy tail. Today a more comic image prevails.

Lucky black cats used to appear at British weddings; embossed cardboard cutouts would be carried by the bride with her bouquet, along with other good luck emblems. They can sometimes be seen in old wedding photographs, and possibly some long-established Old World stationer may still have them in stock.

65

— 65 —

This late 1940s American Halloween lantern of a black cat face, is the hanging type and also electric. It is made from cardboard and paper, two sided and measures 11in × 11in.

66

— 66 —

To celebrate Halloween, this party set from c.1950, consisting of a 40in × 40in table cover and 4 paper napkins, was printed with pumpkins and black cats on orange paper. It is unopened and marked "Made in USA."

— 67 —

This charming pop-up Birthday card drawn by Lustig, was produced by Popshots Inc., of Westport, Connecticut.

— 68 —

Cat calendars are an annual delight and this American one for the year 1987 is known as "The Natural Cat Calendar."

touching photographic records of cats taken in by animal rescue organizations.

At the turn of the century, cat calendars and almanacs were rolling off the presses of both Ernest Nister and Raphael Tuck. In 1899 Tuck moved into splendid new purpose-built premises in London's Moorfields, producing "Christmas cards, calendars, books, engravings and a thousand and one other forms of beautiful decoration"; three of its calendars of this vintage consisted of cardboard cutouts showing cats swinging on a clock pendulum, sitting in a basket, and balancing on a pair of scales. A tantalizing volume of Nister samples for 1896, in mint condition, is preserved in the British Library. Among the many cat calendars in this treasure trove is an amusing feline version of the Royal Academy on opening day: not only are the visitors all portrayed as dressed-up cats, but the exhibits, too, have been transformed so that Millais' *Bubbles* becomes a gray kitten, and Cupid and Psyche are statuesque white cats.

The same sort of transformation, incidentally, but on a wider canvas, has been worked almost a century later by Susan Herbert whose *Cats' Gallery of Art* has amused and delighted present-day cat-lovers, and whose *Victorian Cats* are to grace a 1993 calendar.

Another annual delight is the *Cats in Art* diary published by Alan Hutchison, each volume containing a superb reproduction for every week of the year. The compilers have searched world-wide for little-known cat portraits and have included a Roman mosaic, stained glass, and needlework, as well as hundreds of drawings and paintings. Whether or not you actually keep a diary, *Cats in Art* is an essential purchase.

— 69 —
This Valentine card with a cat motif is American and measures 3¾in × 3¾in.

Cats are a popular decorative motif no matter what the holiday. Valentine, Easter, and patriotic holiday postcards from the golden era, 1898 to 1918, often utilized a cat as the central decorative motif. American valentines remain a favorite home for felines.

Greeting cards for birthdays, new homes, convalescence, and every other eventuality and occasion include some excellent cat portraits and are a means of publicizing the work of many interesting contemporary artists. Ditz, Joan Freestone,

Susan Herbert, and Thaddeus Krumeich are just four out of scores of artists whose cats can be collected through greeting cards.

Cats must outnumber all other animals as decorations for sheets of gift wrapping paper and festive shopping bags, and collectors should not ignore this new source of cat-related ephemera. The most attractive of the gift bags come from Alan Hutchison , whose glossy carriers are decorated with portraits by Stubbs (Miss White's Kitten) and Walter

Lolita by Thaddeus Krumeich has been reproduced as a greeting card, c.1980. The integral "wooden" frame is a characteristic of Krumeich's work.

Crane. Other publishers have produced bags with cats by Henriette Ronner and Alan Cracknell. As for sheets of wrapping paper, they are still amazingly cheap in relation to the quality of the printing: years ago I framed a Sarah Bowman tabby sitting among flowers and, completely unfaded, it is still giving great pleasure. Karin Van Heerden's *Peaceable Kingdom,* full of cats large and small, is awaiting the same treatment.

Cats
Through
The Post

— 71 —

The highly prolific
French artist Maurice
Boulanger designed
this postcard
displaying the "upper
body" of a cat, and a
cat wearing a green
hat. It is part of the
series no. 116 and is
$3\frac{7}{8}$in × $5\frac{3}{4}$in.

Collecting cat postcards is another field wide enough to occupy an enthusiast's full-time attention. Picture-postcards date from 1870; at first one whole side of the card was reserved for the address and any message had to be written on the same side as the picture. In 1902, however, the British postal authorities agreed that the front of the card could be given over completely to the picture and the back divided between message and address. Almost overnight, a flood of new cards appeared, and a new collecting fever had taken hold.

Since cat pictures were now more popular than ever, it is only to be expected that they were used on so many early 20th-century cards. Among the artists who drew cats for the postcard trade, Louis Wain, of course, stands supreme in the collecting world. In 1902 Raphael Tuck published a children's book *Pa Cats,*

Ma Cats and their Kittens with Wain illustrations, and almost immediately they re-used at least three of the pictures on postcards, showing cats dining at a table, three cats on a swing, and three kittens having a bath. Both Raphael Tuck and Ernest Nister made full use of their artists' work, constantly recycling book illustrations for postcards and calendars. In fact, so many of Louis Wain's drawings were re-used in this way that in 1903 he toyed with the idea of printing a series of postcards himself, but his business sense was never very strong and he seems soon to have abandoned the project.

Publishers of Louis Wain cards include Tuck, Faulkner, Valentine, Wrench, Hartmann, Davidson, and Nister. Between 1907 and early 1910, he was in the U.S., and during this time, he produced yet more cat drawings for postcard manufacturers. Cards of this period were often made even more attractive by em-

This greeting card, "You Are A Dear," c.1900, shows a kitten in a slipper on the front and opens to reveal a full-length portrait of the kitten without the slipper.

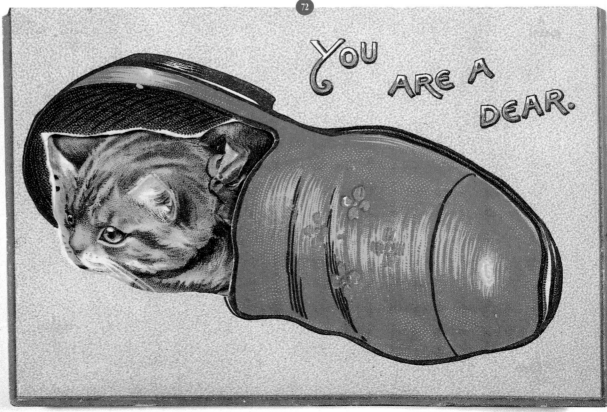

English, or German titles, it shows cats driving cars, playing Blind Man's Buff, attending a wedding, bicycling, and engaging in other lively human-like pursuits. There are twelve cards in the set, published in England by Henry Moss & Co. and printed, as were so many cards of this period, in Austria. Boulanger's cats are recognizable by their long, spiky whiskers, their smiles, and their expressive, triangular eyes (see page 55).

— 73 —

This postcard signed by the artist Louis Wain is postmarked 1906 and bears the trademark of Osborne Post Cards of New York, but printed in England.

bossing them in a process giving extra depth to an illustration. To list all his postcards would be a mammoth (and probably impossible) task: there are cats both dressed and undressed, cats at Christmas, and cats on the beach – cats, in fact, of every imaginable sort. To the uninitiated, the prices being asked for these cards may seem astronomical; but from a collector's point of view, Louis Wain is in a class of his own.

However, there are many other artists to consider. Arthur Thiele (dates are uncertain, but he is thought to have been born in Dresden, Germany, in 1841) was drawing animals for postcards from the late 1890s onward, and his cats in particular have great charm. Most have good-natured, round, kitten-type faces and are beautifully dressed, with lady-cats displaying the latest fashions. The Nuremburg firm of Theo Stroefer published almost all of Thiele's cat cards, though many were reproduced by Tuck for the British market.

Maurice Boulanger was a French artist who added greatly to the number of early 20th-century postcard cats. He was responsible for several series or sets of cards which today's collectors go to a lot of trouble to complete; apparently, the easiest set to find is the "In Catland" series. Issued with either French,

— 74 —

A postcard showing two tabbies in a carriage drawn by two larger ginger-and-white cats was printed in Germany and mailed in England in 1904.

— 75 —

This typical Arthur Thiele postcard, showing charming, well-dressed cats, displays the words "You ought to see the other fellow," and measures 3½in × 5½in.

Collectors of cats in general who may be unfamiliar with postcards of this early period could "get their eye in" by studying the illustrations in *Cat Country,* a small book with text by Joan Tate (Ram Publishing Company, 1979), as the story is woven around twenty early cat cards. Eleven of them are unmistakably by Boulanger; one, showing cats around a Christmas tree, has "1906" inked in after the printed greeting and bears the famous Tuck trademark. Four of the others actually carry Arthur Thiele's signature, and another interesting inclusion

is an American card copyrighted in 1907 by Albert Hahn of New York, showing three cats driving in the Catskills.

Anthropomorphic, dressed-up cats were what the public looked for when buying cards by Wain, Thiele, and Boulanger, but plenty of other artists specialized in more natural-looking animals for the postcard trade. One of the most successful and prolific was Helena Maguire, a member of a family of artists, who had already made her name with designs for Christmas cards in the 1880s. She

CATS ON STAMPS

~

Cats on postage stamps are a major subject in themselves. Some years ago, it was estimated that, since the mid-1950s, 115 different countries had put cats on their stamps, and by now the number has probably increased; Poland issued a series of cat portraits in 1964, and other complete sets of domestic cats have been produced by Korea (1983), Nicaragua (1984), Guinea and Kampuchea (both 1985). Puss-in-Boots appeared in Hungary in 1960 and in East Germany in 1968; in the same year John Dawson designed commemorative cat stamps for the United States. In Great Britain, Edward Lear's drawing of a cat has been used on a stamp, as has Tenniel's grinning Cheshire Cat from Alice in Wonderland. A tabby kitten was chosen to mark the 150th anniversary of royal patronage of the Royal Society for the Prevention of Cruelty to Animals in 1990.

— 76 —

A sheetlet of six East German Puss-in-Boots stamps, issued in 1968.

— 77 —

A block of four U.S. cat stamps has two cat heads per jumbo commemorative stamp, all designed by John Dawson and issued on February 5, 1988.

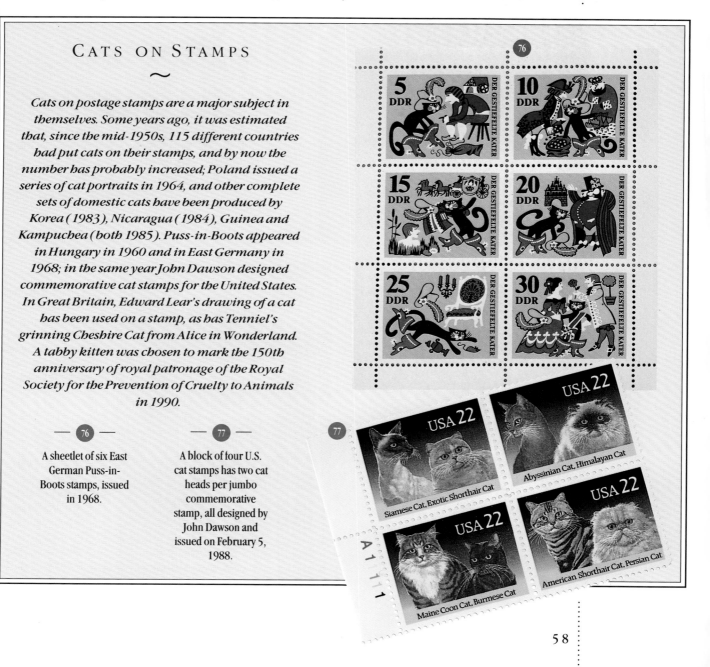

This postcard, which is 5½in × 3½in and signed S. Sperlich, shows five kittens and is part of series no. 1002. It was printed in Germany.

produced hundreds of watercolors of fluffy cats and kittens in domestic surroundings, sometimes in natural positions, more often occupied with human activities – but never wearing clothes. Other artists among the creators of "fluffy" postcard cats are G. Vernon Stokes, T. Sperlich, B. Cobbe, M. Scrivener, C. Reichert, and Rosa Bebb, but many cards lack any mention of the artist's name, and positive identification is often impossible.

Another category of cat postcard features photographs of real animals. The best-known of the early animal photographers was Landor, who supplied countless studies of carefully posed cats; they ride in miniature wheelbarrows or trains, sit in a doll's cradle suspended from a tree, parachute among the stars, and perform scenes from nursery rhymes. "Landor's Cat Studies" were published by several firms, including Rotary Photographic, Raphael Tuck, and Wrench; the earliest in my own collection is postmarked 1902. These photographic cards – some tinted – are still priced at a comparatively low level; little has been written about them, and it would be an interesting project for a collector to try to complete the sets published by the major firms. In addition to the Landor studies, I have some of the colored Tuck "Rapholette Glosso" series S137 entitled *Teddy's*

SWING HIGH, SWING LOW.   E. LANDOR. (COPYRIGHT.)

Displaying a typical Landor cat which is very posed, this card is entitled "Swing High, Swing Low," and measures 5⅜in × 3⁷⁄₁₆in.

AMERICAN ART

FROM THE NATIONAL GALLERY OF ART

— 80 —

A box of note cards bought in 1986 contains reproductions of 19th-century paintings in the collections of the National Gallery of Art in Washington, DC. The cat group is dated 1872/83.

Little Love Affair, chronicling a romance between a teddy bear and two kittens (postmarked 1928); in 1908 the British firm M. & A. Austin of St. Albans had issued *The Romantic Love Story of Blackie & Beauty: A Comedy in 12 Scenes.*

The most popular American artist of this special *genre* must surely be Harry Whittier Frees, whose comic photographs of dressed-up cats appeared on postcards in the U.S., Britain, and in Europe from 1905 until about 1960. He was born in Reading, Pennsylvania, in 1879, and by the time his photographic career began in the early 1900s, picture postcards were at the height of their popularity, and his clever studies of dogs and cats were much in demand. An English collector, Mrs. Anne R. Bradford, set out to discover more about him, gathering information from booksellers in the United States and from postcard fairs and clubs, and in 1977 she published privately her tribute – *The Animal Magic of Harry Whittier Frees.* He had, she found, begun giving his animal sitters

THE BAD GIRL OF.THE FAMILY!

— 81 —

This reproduction of a design by Violet Roberts, "The Bad Girl of the Family," is by Mayfair Cards of London and measures 4⅛in × 6in.

small pieces of clothing around 1905, but later costumes were much more elaborate; made by his mother, the outfits included slacks which allowed the animals to be posed in an upright posture, nightclothes for them to wear at bedtime, and even fancy costumes. A selection of Frees cards is reproduced in Mrs. Bradford's book.

She also reprints an article from a 1925 issue of *Little Folks* describing his methods: every picture, readers were assured, was genuine, the animals were never intimidated or forced to endure rigorous training, and they certainly appear thoroughly to enjoy being dressed up and having their pictures taken. The star performer was Rags, an ordinary short-haired tabby-and-white with remarkable intelligence and good nature, and his well-loved portrait appeared on millions of cards worldwide.

Sadly, Mrs. Bradford learned that Frees died in tragic circumstances, almost destitute and something of a recluse, in 1953.

SEASIDE CATS
~

Seaside cats played a large part in the postcard world, appealing as they did to vacationers who despatched cards by the million to family and friends at home. Louis Wain delighted in drawing cats on the beach or getting out of bathing machines; around 1912, postcards by a less celebrated artist, Violet Roberts (who was in fact a professional singer), came onto the market. She, too, favored cats grouped around bathing machines and produced some lively pictures of kittens riding donkeys along the sand. William Ellam, working for various publishers including Raphael Tuck from 1905 onward, drew comical pairs of cats or dogs having breakfast in bed, with a notice hanging above the bedhead announcing that this luxury is "charged extra"; the card in my collection has been overprinted with the claim that "Minehead's the place for a jolly rest cure," a useful device for linking a popular illustration with a particular resort.

Valentine's published an equally adaptable card, featuring a fine black cat standing on an embroidered red pouffe and printed with the words "Good Luck from . . . ." The name of a seaside town could be added as

82

Published by Valentines in the early 20th century, this fold-out postcard features Lucky Black Cat and brings greetings and twelve photographic views from Tintagel, the wild Cornish beauty spot associated with the legend of King Arthur.

83

Breakfast in Bed Charged Extra: a postcard designed by Ellam for Raphael Tuck's Oilette series. This card was mailed in 1911.

82

— 84 —

These four postcards are typical of those sold at Atlantic Ocean beach resorts during the 1950s. They are all published by "Colour-picture" from Cambridge, Massachusetts.

— 85 —

The photograph on this postcard, printed in Germany c.1910 shows a cat with added glass eyes, ribbon bows, and a felt mouse.

series, consisting of simple outline drawings for children to color, and at the other end of the scale the *Oil-facsim* range ("the last word . . . veritable art gem showing the actual brush-marks of the Artist and indistinguishable from the Original Painting"). By 1910, the firm had inaugurated an Exchange Register, inviting collectors to add their names so that they could exchange postcards with correspondents all over the world. Thus they would secure "a really valuable collection of artistic Postcards addressed to themselves, stamped and complete with the postmark of the respective towns and countries."

required, but the really ingenious selling point was that the central portion of the card lifted up to reveal a series of twelve views of the same resort, folded in an accordion strip.

There were dozens more novelty cards to tempt buyers; photographs of cats were made more interesting by having glass eyes – blue or green – added, and a narrow ribbon bow. I have one with the cat holding a mouse made of felt, and another which squeaks when pressed. Raphael Tuck issued a *Paintbox*

— 86 —

Out for Luck: Another lucky black cat postcard, this one, c.1925, is from Raphael Tuck's Oilette series.

OUT FOR LUCK!

WOODEN
CATS

87

— 87 —

An alert carved and
painted American
"calico" cat, perhaps
originally used as a
doorstop, a toy, or to
commemorate a
family pet. Made
around 1900–1920.
It measures 21in ×
8in × 5in. (Abby
Aldridge Rockefeller
Folk Art Center.)

Carvings of cats have been found on the elaborate medieval woodwork of European cathedrals and churches going back to the 14th century and perhaps beyond. But these are "collectible" only in the sense that they can be sought out, marveled at, and – with permission – photographed. The earliest European wooden cats to have become collectors' items probably began as simple playthings made to amuse children in peasant communities long before the days of industrialization. The great pine forests of southern Germany provided abundant raw material and the long winters plenty of time, and over the years domestic woodcarving and toymaking evolved into a commercial undertaking with an organized market. Noah's Arks were invariably given a pair of cats, and the original German bellows toys – later successfully copied in North America – often represented mewing cats.

German toys were being exported in considerable quantities by 1800, but so, too, were the skills that produced them. European immigrants crossing the Atlantic carried their traditional crafts with them; and by the second half of the 19th century, Pennsylvania in particular had a thriving woodcarving industry. Most Pennsylvania cats are characterized by bright spots with contrasting colors for feet, tail, and collar, though some were given natural coloring. Decorative wooden cats of every kind are of course still being made all over the world, and collectors are again faced with an almost bewildering choice.

Among the hundreds of remarkable cats shown at Salisbury Museum's 1991 Exhibition in England were two late 20th-century limewood cat models from Brienz, Switzerland's woodcarving center in the Bernese Oberland. These carvings were the work of Hans Aebischer, an artist who loves cats and who has captured,

— 88 —

Made in Switzerland probably in the 1930s, this carved wooden cat dozes in a crouching position.

88

89

— 89 —

A Japanese cherrywood carving dates from the late 18th century. The cat tears fiercely at a box containing a rat, and the model is signed *Tametake* on the base. Its height is 1¾in.

with these two, the movement of one animal stretching just after waking, and the repose of the other, curled up asleep.

In the same exhibition there were cats on loan from Mrs. Langton's fabulous collection. These included a late 18th-century Japanese cherry-wood *netsuke* considered by experts to be one of her finest treasures; a small masterpiece only 1¾ inches (4.5cm) high, the carving is of a furious cat tearing at a box with a rat inside it. From the Nagoya school, it is signed by the artist Tametaka. Another Japanese model, this time from the late 19th century, is a pear-wood carving of a cat with two kittens, all sitting upright with left paws raised in the traditional Japanese greeting. Cats in this beckoning attitude (known as Maneki-neko) are still made in the Far East and widely exported; they are often seen in gift shops, made from a material that could be a modern wood resin. With their naïve charm, they are collectible at the right price.

Antique wooden dummy boards found in British and American 18th and 19th-century homes and made to represent life-size figures both human and animal, sometimes featured cats. Painted in natural colors and cut from a flat piece of wood, they were used as free-standing decorations and, some suggest, to deter intruders. Writing in 1673, the British diarist John Evelyn mentions an entertainment in London's Hatton Garden "furnished with the representations of all sorts of animals, handsomely painted on boards or cloth & so cut out & made to stand and move ... as was not unpretty." By the 19th century, English dummy board animals were evidently quite common; visitors to Tunbridge Wells, for example, could buy collage pictures and cutout figures made by G.

— 90 —

A late 19th-century Japanese pearwood carving shows three cats, all sitting upright with left paws raised in traditional welcome. It is signed on the base O-en, or Cherry Garden, the name of the workshop.

90

91

Two American hand-crafted and painted wooden cats sit on rugs. These country-style cats were made by Natalie Silitch,, Annapolis, MD, and were bought in a Pennsylvania Farmers' Market in 1973.

Smart, described as an "artist in cloth and velvet." An engraving of 1840 shows rows of cats and other animal shapes displayed outside his shop, with customers inspecting them. In England, York Museum has a dummy-board dated 1871 showing a charming little seated cat, and an article published at the same period in the learned Journal of the British Archaeological Association refers to older boards representing dogs, cats, and parrots.

Chimney boards could be described as dummy boards with a specific purpose. As the name implies, they were made to fit into a fireplace opening to hide the empty grate during the summer. The decorations on these boards were not cut out, but occupied a rectangular or square space much like a conventional painting. There are numerous 18th-century references to chimney boards (also called fire boards or chimney stops), and the French artist Jean Baptiste Oudry painted one with a very aristocratic-looking dog. A particularly interesting board now in Washington's Cooper-Hewitt Museum was covered with a piece of French wallpaper (c.1830) portraying a Persian cat surrounded by flowers, fruit, and birds.

TYBER KATZ

~

"Tyber Katz," the models created by Americans Peter and Pat Tyber, are really collectors' items, although there is a delightful toy-like quality about them. Each cat has head and paws hand-carved by Peter Tyber from Oregon pine. The cats are then hand-painted, horsehair whiskers are attached, and they are beautifully dressed in silk and other fine fabrics; every cat is unique and part of a limited-edition set.

— 93 —

A group of Tyber *Prairie Katz and Kittens* described as belonging to the studio's most affordable editions, are limited to 350 and 150 respectively. Prairie Katz are 16in high; Kittens are 10in.

— 92 —

Pat and Peter Tyber's models combine the charm of both cat and doll worlds. Head and paws of each limited-edition cat are hand-carved from basswood or pine and then meticulously hand-painted. This is the original Tyber *Fat Kat.* Fat Kat is 22in tall with movable arms and horsehair whiskers, and wears a custom-designed sweater.

Today a collector would be fortunate to find an antique dummy or chimney board. In the 1980s, however, the idea of the dummy board was revived; and cats, dogs, and baskets of fruit and flowers became great favorites with interior decorators. Some artists have specialized in cutout portraits of individual pets, usually working from photographs, and cat-lovers might consider adding an example to their collection. Maggie Howard is an English artist whose work is popular on both sides of the Atlantic; she paints dogs and cats to order, interpreting traditional dummy boards through the modern medium of acrylics on five-ply wood.

Cat versions of traditional nesting dolls qualify as decorative pieces rather than toys. The turned wooden figures come apart to reveal smaller and smaller cats wearing variously colored coats; they are not entirely successful since the production method means the ears have to be flat and are merely painted onto the rounded head. Nesting dolls are of course associated with Russian toy-making, but I have never found a set of these cats with any indication of the country of origin. They appear to be quite recent arrivals from the Far East.

In the days before pet stores were full of specially designed beds for animals, cats were well-known for taking over comfortable pieces of dolls' furniture. A kitten asleep in a miniature cradle or four-poster is very appealing; it is a picture that has been used over and over again by artists and photographers. "Daisy in Dolly's Crib" appeared as an engraving in the magazine *St. Nicholas* in 1874, and Harry Whittier Frees seems to have had no difficulty in persuading his cat models to lie down in dolls' beds, actually dressing them in nightclothes first. Beautifully made dolls' beds, complete with original bedclothes and draperies, do occasionally come onto the market, and a typically lavish Victorian example would make a striking addition to a collection of cat-related antiques. The Museum of Miniature Furniture at the Château de Vendeuvre in Normandy, France, uses a photograph of a magnificent ginger-and-white cat stretched out on a canopied *bateau-lit* to illustrate its publicity material.

Wooden houses for cats make unusual items to collect, as long as there is room for them. I have an

95

indoor cat "kennel," attractively finished with Dutch gables and raised up on feet to guard against drafts. It has the look of the late 19th century, but unfortunately it came to me without any provenance. I think, though, it must be haunted by some feline ghost – none of my cats will voluntarily go inside it.

American designers have given cats a wide choice of desirable residences, based on castles, chapels, barns, and cottages to suit all tastes. A company called Animal Manors has constructed, among other elaborate buildings, a scaled-down Persian temple and a Spanish colonial mansion.

I was doubtful about mentioning carousel cats, the most spectacular of wooden cats. I was afraid they were so rare as to be virtually uncollectible, but in my scrapbooks I have found photographs of four of these lively creatures. The one in the Abby Aldrich Rockefeller Folk Art Collection in Williamsburg, Virginia, once part of an amusement park in Seattle, dates from around 1905. It has a fish in its mouth, and except for its coloring and the details of its elaborate harness, it looks identical to the one, often seen in a photograph, in Cecile Singer's collection. At least two other merry-go-round cats crossed the Atlantic and used to delight visitors to Lady Bangor's Fairground Collection at Wookey Hole, Somerset, England. One is black, with a mouse in its mouth, the other white.

— 96 —

This indoor kennel for a cat was probably specially made for a beloved pet. The sturdy, natural-looking toy cat is one of Sylvia King's creations, made to order in 1991.

96

METAL
CATS

97

— 97 —

This cat sitting on a
cast-iron egg is a
child's bank. There is
a hole for money on
the cat's back; as the
coins drop in, the
chick's head moves.
Made between 1880
and 1900, probably
in the U.S.

From iron doorstops to silver spoons and from ancient Egyptian bronzes to Benares brass, metal cats come in a thousand shapes and sizes. For the serious collector, there are exquisite English enamel boxes made in Battersea or Bilston in the reign of George III, cats cast in bronze from the celebrated French *animaliers* of the 19th century, and modern jewelry set with precious stones; at the other extreme are cheap little objects to be bought on impulse – decorated canisters, ballpoint pens with oriental cats in imitation cloisonné, cat-shaped cookie cutters, keyrings, and dozens more.

Of course, given the chance of acquiring a Georgian enamel snuff-box decorated with a cat, few collectors could resist at least considering the matter carefully. Wolverhampton Museum possesses two small round boxes to inspire cat-lovers to search for others: both date from 1770–80, one being a patch box with its lid stamped and painted to represent a striped tabby amid scrollwork, the other with a similar lying-down cat, but painted to look like a tortoise-shell on a pink cushion. Mrs. Langton's collection includes an even more entrancing example – a *bonbonnière* (a miniature candy box) molded in the form of a reclining cat with brown and black painted markings. Written beneath the tiny tabby playing the part of the British Lion is the patriotic verse that gives this piece its special charm:

May Britain's Sons
For ever be,
A Conquering People
Loved & Free

To most collectors, an object of this caliber would represent a substantial investment, and a buyer would need to be sure that the price was justified. As with purchases of antique ceramics, it is advisable to build up a relationship with a reliable dealer before spending a great deal of money.

— 98 —

Two Japanese bronze cats. The cat lying down dates from the late 1800s, while the seated one is modern, bought in about 1980 from Gumps in San Francisco, California.

98

— 99 —

An English enamel bonbonniere dish from the late 18th century, just over 1in high, probably made at Bilston in Staffordshire, England, is molded in the form of a cat lying down. It has a patriotic verse on the lid.

Recently several firms have revived the original enameling methods used at Battersea and Bilston and have produced some delightful small boxes. A number of them feature cats, either modeled in low relief for the *bonbonnière* type of container, or painted on a flat round or oval lid. They can be found in places selling rather expensive gifts, with the best selection in Europe probably still at Halcyon Days, the London firm which pioneered the revival.

From time to time, some wonderful cats appear at auction, as they did in December 1984 when a unique

— 100 —

A typical example of an Austrian bronze, c.1900, showing three cats eating a Christmas pudding. It is based on the card behind it; designed by Helen Maguire.

101

101

A pair of late 19th-century Viennese bronze cat "busts." Named by their present owner "My Cat's Ancestors," they are rare examples of small Austrian bronzes which are extremely popular with collectors. Height 2¾in.

collection of miniature painted bronzes were sold in London. The cats, two hundred of them, had been made in Austria between 1880 and 1920; they included little figures engaged in all sorts of human and feline activities: there were billiard-players, a policeman, mothers with kittens, skaters, an artist at his easel, kite-flyers, and Red Riding Hood among them, and an enthusiastic crowd turned up to bid. In virtually every case, the price realized was far higher than the auctioneer's estimate; even so, the cats have no doubt proved good investments as these small Austrian bronzes are understandably very popular.

Little seems to be known about their manufacture. They are generally referred to as Austrian or Viennese bronzes, though other metal compositions were also used. Mrs. Flora Gill Jacobs has a rare pair of portrait busts which she calls "My Cat's Ancestors" which are greatly admired

102

These miniature jointed cat toys by Hantel (English, c.1985) are cast in pewter and hand-painted. The Puss-in-Boots figure stands only 1⅓in high.

by visitors to her Dolls' House and Toy Museum in Washington, D.C. In December 1892, a London shop was advertising "novelties for presents" and singled out a bronze pug-dog sandwich-board man carrying Christmas and New Year greetings (there is a cat version, too) and a cat and mouse bookmark; they cost half a crown each; at the time this price would have made them luxury goods.

Modern miniatures with comparable minute detailing come from Hantel, a British firm that began to make models for dolls' houses in 1980. Working strictly to a scale of 1:12, Hantel's designer produced a line of playthings intended for dolls' house families, but the cat toys are collectible in their own right. Made of pewter, an ideal medium for casting detailed objects of this size, the cat figures include the Owl and the Pussycat in their Peagreen Boat, a delightful Puss-in-Boots looking like a pantomime character, and a pretty white cat "doll." Their prices put them in the category of adult toys.

Cast-iron banks (money-boxes) in the form of cats were popular in 19th-century America, and a great many have survived. Probably their weight made them uneconomic to ship overseas in any quantity, and genuine examples are not easy to find in Europe, but there are innumerable British-made cast-iron andirons for the hearth and door-stops representing cats. Cast-iron figures were quite cheap to produce, and from the mid-19th century onward, they were manufactured in their thousands; some, like the doorstops, served a useful purpose, while others seem to have been purely decorative. A lifelike cat sitting on a plinth was designed to hold a ball of string inside its body, with the end of the string coming through a hole in its side; this is an unusual

103

— 103 —

This cast-iron cat figure is fitted with hooks at the back to hold fire-irons. It has been suggested that the design for this elegant feline originated in France, but this model was registered in England in the early 20th century.

and highly desirable model. The majority of cast-iron cats are the archetypal rounded animals, sitting bolt upright and gazing straight ahead; a more sinuous model, fitted with hooks at the back for hanging hearth implements, makes an interesting change. This cat, with glass eyes and a floppy bow around its neck, is often described as 19th century, but a careful examination of the base reveals an official Design Registry number showing it could not have been made much before 1910. The manufacturer's name is given as Nestor. Victorian doorstops are now being reproduced; some very attractive ones come from the Ironbridge Gorge Museum in England and are clearly labeled as replicas of originals in the museum's collection.

Groups and single animals modeled by the French *animaliers* are known to have been cast in iron as well as the more usual and expensive bronze. Pierre-Jules Mêne (1810–79) modeled lovely, natural-looking cats that are great favorites with collectors, especially his mother-and-kittens group; a pair of Mêne foxhounds was cast in iron at Coalbrookdale, and a determined search might uncover Mêne cats in this metal.

Brass cat-related items are legion; as one keen collector has remarked, most brass cats seem to come from either England or India, and it is often impossible to be absolutely sure about their date or provenance. Prices are still modest, and second-hand dealers can usually offer a selection of brass-topped toasting forks featuring cats, cat-shaped ashtrays (a rather charming one has a notice reading "Born Blind" suspended around the cat's neck) door knockers, horse brasses (but beware of fakes), and bottle openers. Shining brass models, anonymous but almost certainly from the Far East, are to be seen everywhere in gift stores and street markets.

Metal cat bird-scarers are a quaint survival from long-forgotten gardens. Made of iron, they consist of a cat's head in silhouette, with nose and whiskers punched out and eyes filled with glass marbles that glint alarmingly in the sun. They are said to have originated in France about 1900, but an enterprising English firm has reintroduced a simplified version, marketed as "Grandad's Old-fashioned Bird Scarer." Cat weather-

— 104 —

A brass ashtray in the form of a kitten sits on three brass feet. The "Born Blind" placard harks back to a well-worn joke: all cats (and dogs) are of course born blind, whether or not they are begging.

104

— 105 —

Two bird-scarer cats are designed to be hung in trees or bushes to protect fruit or newly planted seeds. The model with the cutout mouth and whiskers is early 20th century, while the simpler model is modern, made in England. Both models have eyes made of marbles which glint in the sun.

vanes are uncommon, but not completely unknown; an example in New England will probably be familiar to many collectors through photographs.

Decorated canisters manufactured exclusively for firms in the confectionery trade now form a specialized collecting field (see Advertising and Packaging chapter). Far easier to find, and at a fraction of the price, are small cat-decorated tins produced in more recent years. New designs are constantly coming onto the market, some large enough to use as teacaddies, while others can serve to hold pins, pills, or postage stamps. Some of the most original are made by Hunkdory, an English company that obviously understands the pulling power of cat collectibles. This

firm markets an ever-growing line of Lesley Ann Ivory's designs, including attractive cottage-style buildings with cats perched in the windows. They also made smaller boxes with dog and cat shapes stamped in relief on the hinged lids, in the manner of a Georgian enamel snuffbox. These remarkable pieces were designed by Dana Kubick and are dated 1984; two years later, the same partnership between artist and manufacturer offered even more striking cats in three dimensions, divided vertically into front and back sections and oddly reminiscent of Egyptian mummy cases. In 1990 there were small round boxes with an animal printed on the lid and its young (including kittens) printed on the inside of the base.

— 106 —

This ceramic-headed cat doll, made in Taiwan, presides over a display of small English cat-decorated storage containers purchased during the 1980s.

Beatrix Potter's famous cats appear on assorted boxes and canisters, as do the elegant black felines of Sue Boettcher; nostalgic groups of comic kittens taken from vintage Nister book illustrations have been used to decorate boxes from a different source, unfortunately without any trace of a maker's name.

A true chocolate-box tabby, sitting in a basket, is portrayed on a tin Easter egg, one of a group of beautifully printed eggs designed by Ian Logan and made in Switzerland. Mine still has its price label on it – if only I had had the foresight to buy a dozen. A few years ago they were for sale everywhere, but now a collector would really have to search to find one.

Another recent Easter tin, this one dated 1985 and made in Hong Kong for Schackman, has the well-known Kitty Cucumber and other cats printed on the oval lid and around the sides. It has a carrying handle and a money slot in the top.

— 107 —

A tin Easter bank with a carrying handle is decorated with Kitty Cucumber cat figures. It was made in Hong Kong for B. Shackman & Co. Inc. of New York in 1985. The tin Easter egg, decorated with a tabby kitten, was made in Switzerland in the 1980s from an Ian Logan design.

— 108 —

A silver-plated Victorian napkin ring with a sitting cat forming part of the design. It measures 3½in × 2⅞in.

Silver spoons fall into another class of cat collectible. Spoons with a grinning Cheshire Cat at the end of the handle are obvious souvenirs for collectors visiting Chester in England. In the United States, the famous Salem witch spoon, with the witch's cat lurking at the base of the handle, was made by the Gorham Company; the same firm made souvenir spoons for visitors to the Catskill Mountains, showing two cats fighting. Christening gifts for babies include silver spoons, mugs, rattles, and whistles all decorated with cats.

European collectors envy American friends their heritage of cats cast in Britannia metal. In the 1880s, the Meriden Britannia Company made wonderful silver-plated cats for the dining table, providing feline salt and pepper shakers, knife rests, and, best of all, napkin rings. These everyday objects were transformed by having cats sitting or standing beside them, climbing over them, or carrying them on their backs. One very striking and sought-after napkin ring, by William Rogers, has both a dog and a cat attached to it.

— 107 —

CATS IN TEXTILES

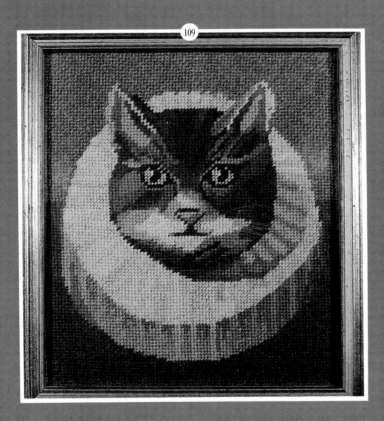

109

— 109 —

A very talented
needle-woman
worked this
handsome cat in a
ruff, based on a
painting by F.
Diehlman and its
chromolithograph
reproduction by L.
Prang and Company
of 1875. The picture
was embroidered in
the 1970s.

A famous cat embroidered by Mary Queen of Scots hangs in the room where she slept in Edinburgh's Palace of Holyrood. Of course, a 16th-century needlework cat of any kind, let alone a royal one, is a great rarity, and today's collectors would be fortunate if they found even an 18th-century example outside a museum. The Metropolitan Museum of Art in New York possesses an early American sampler with two fairly recognizable cats sewn by Patty Goodeshall, who was born in 1780. In Europe these embroidered panels, designed primarily to teach a variety of useful and decorative stitches, had been worked by young girls as part of their education since the early 17th century. By the mid-1600s a scattering of pictorial motifs, including animals, had been added to the repertory of basic stitches, and a finely worked linen panel of about 1650 in the Victoria and Albert Museum, London, does in fact portray a quite cat-like and tame-looking leopard. Later examples from the 1800s in this museum's unrivalled collection feature many small creatures, including domestic cats. Samplers of this period are not difficult to find, and from time to time an auction house will put them into a general sale of antique textiles.

An embroidered sampler by a Welsh child named Sarah Davies incorporates a fine tabby cat as its centerpiece. Unlike many samplers, this one is undated, but probably belongs to the mid-19th century. Translated into English the verse reads, "Let not your heart despair, you believe in God, believe in me also."

111

However, most sampler cats tend to be flat and insignificant, playing only a minor part in an overall design. They were succeeded by far more imposing animals, lifelike and even lifesize, that could be worked from the colored charts that took Europe by storm in the mid-19th century. Developed in Germany about 1810, Berlin woolwork, as this new form of cross-stitch embroidery was called, entailed no more than transposing ready-made designs from squared charts to squared canvas. Given time and patience, anybody could achieve acceptable results. The craze reached its height in the 1840s, by which time over 14,000 different patterns had been imported into England alone. The Victorian love of all things feline was reflected in the number of cat charts available: leisured ladies with time on their hands could choose from a gallery of contented tabbies curled up on tasseled pillows, mothers and kittens in baskets, alert little creatures sitting upright, and dozens more. The finished work was incorporated into upholstery or used for throw-pillows, firescreens, or pictures – particularly attractive in maplewood frames. All these cats are highly collectible, but those with their fur worked in a raised "plush" stitch, with the wool cut to give a rich velvet texture, have a special cachet.

Prompted by the present-day interest in Victorian work, several designers have recreated cats in the same style. Elizabeth Bradley's two patterns for cats (one fat, one thin) have been great successes in both Europe and the U.S. Kaffe Fassett is an outstanding textile designer whose many brilliant creations include a pair of tabby kittens posed against a lace pillow. All three designs can be bought as kits complete with canvas, chart, and wool, to give cat-

— 111 —

A woolwork cat on a red tasseled pillow. This cat's "fur" is embroidered in a special "plush" stitch, probably by a professional, giving it an effective three-dimensional look.

lovers many hours of pleasant occupation as well as worthwhile additions to their collections.

Erica Wilson's embroidery designs are probably best known in the United States, though she was born in England and studied at the Royal School of Needlework. Among her many cats are "Chessie" and "Peake," mascots of the Chesapeake and Ohio Railroad (see chapter on Advertising Cats), and a trio of tabby kittens in crewel work.

Rugs and fair-sized carpets have been worked in needlepoint and other embroidery stitches; the Metropolitan Museum of Art's renowned "Caswell" carpet, made in Vermont in the early 1830s, has two adjoining panels showing a cat and her kittens, all worked in tambour stitch on a coarse twill-weave wool foundation. Later in the 19th century, the making of hooked or "rag" rugs,

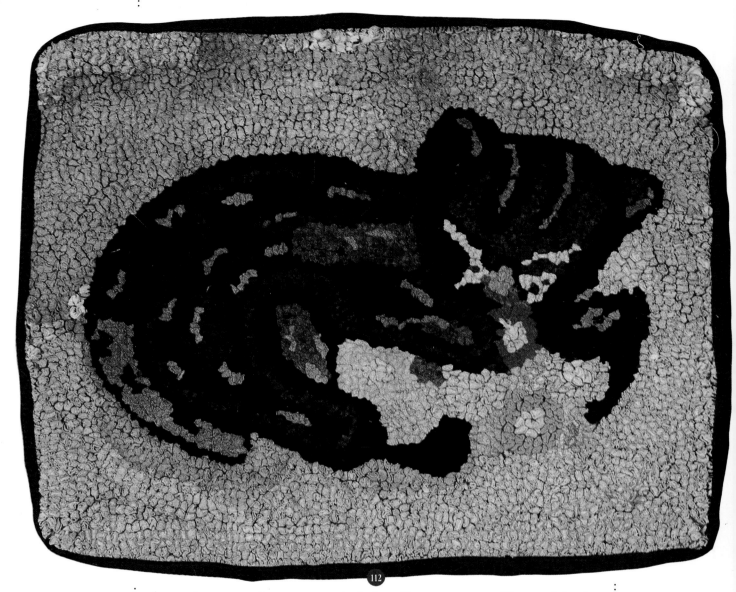

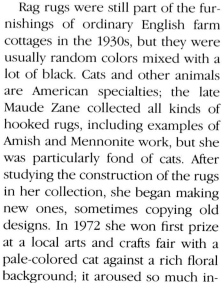

decorative as well as economical, became popular in America. They cost almost nothing, since the materials consisted of discarded garments cut into strips and then hooked into a foundation provided by an old feed sack. Even so, the various colors were carefully arranged in patterns, or to represent flowers, foliage, or animals. No doubt the cozy domestic cat seemed a good subject for a fireside rug, and many family pets must have been immortalized in this way; needless to say, these rugs are eagerly sought, both by private collectors and for display in museums of folk art.

Rag rugs were still part of the furnishings of ordinary English farm cottages in the 1930s, but they were usually random colors mixed with a lot of black. Cats and other animals are American specialties; the late Maude Zane collected all kinds of hooked rugs, including examples of Amish and Mennonite work, but she was particularly fond of cats. After studying the construction of the rugs in her collection, she began making new ones, sometimes copying old designs. In 1972 she won first prize at a local arts and crafts fair with a pale-colored cat against a rich floral background; it aroused so much in-

112

A small American hooked rug features a tabby kitten. It measures 15¼in × 12½in.

terest that she was asked to teach traditional rug-making at the Pennsylvania Farm Museum in Landis Valley. Cats remained the favorite subject for her own rugs, and a collector finding a piece of her work today would have discovered a treasure.

Large cotton squares printed with cats are known to have been made for children's handkerchiefs. Brighton Museum (England) has a late 19th-century example showing various scenes connected with a cats' tea party. Another square, featuring the House That Jack Built, just qualifies as a cat collectible, thanks to The Cat That Caught The Rat and Got Worried by The Dog. Over the years, cats must have appeared on countless yards of cheap cotton for children's pinafores, only to have vanished without a trace. A delightful survival from 1884 is preserved in France's Musée de l'Impression sur Etoffes de Mulhause, showing a child and cat (in the style of Steinlen) playing together.

113

— 113 —

Another American hooked rug is appropriately decorated with a sleeping cat. It is 24¾in by 37in.

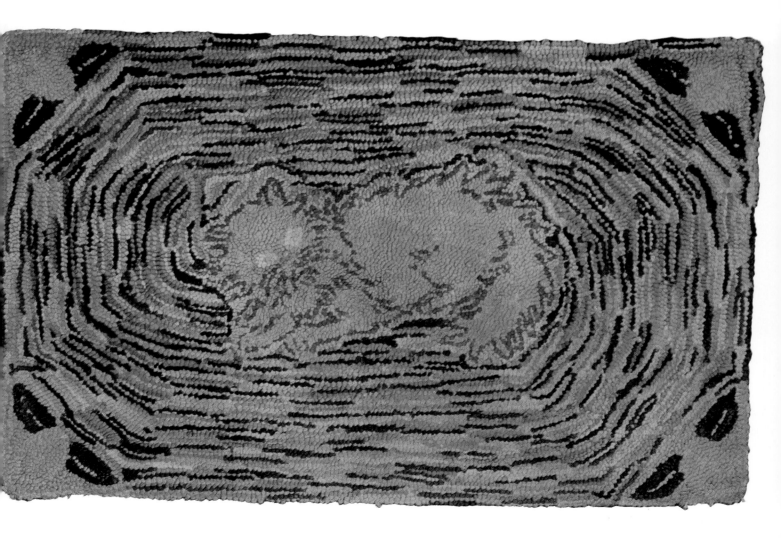

CATS ON QUILTS

~

*The cat appeared occasionally as a secondary
decorative motif in American nineteenth and
early twentieth century quilts. The cat's role
changed during the quilting resurgence of the
American Depression during the late 1920s and
early 1930s. Quilting kits were enormously
popular. Many of these general kits contained
one or more cat theme panels. In many cases, the
pattern was executed as outline embroidery, a
technique that is still popular.*

*Fabrics printed with cats come in enormous
variety. Cotton panels featuring cat motifs were
known as early as the mid-19th century. These
preprinted fabrics, known as cheater's cloth, were
sometimes worked into patchwork quilts. The
present-day popularity of patchwork quilting
has revived the printing of pictorial cottons, and
cats with a folk-art look can sometimes be found
in craft shops. Look for a piece of imprinted cat
motif fabric in an otherwise undistinguished
older quilt at an auction. A surprising number
do turn up.*

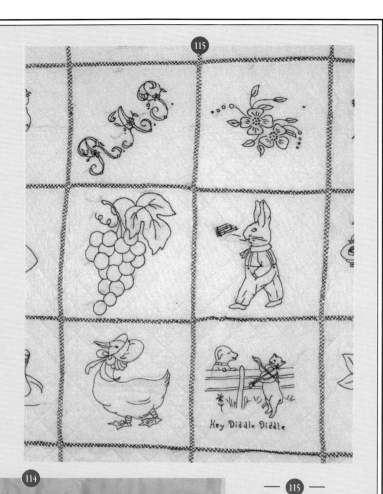

— 114 —

Quilts are very
popular cat items in
the U.S., and shown
here is a pattern
block with a nursery-
type cat from a quilt
made in eastern
Pennsylvania, c.1970.
The entire quilt
measures 40in ×
50in.

114

— 115 —

A section of an
embroidered quilt,
sewn in the early
1940s by Ruth A.
Prosser Kortright,
illustrating the poem,
"Hey Diddle Diddle!"

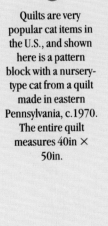

Printed cats of the highest quality can occasionally be found on today's luxury cotton handkerchiefs imported from Switzerland. A collector who showed me a dozen or more remarked that she measured inflation by the price she had to pay when she bought a new one every Christmas in the same store. A tabby cat playing with a butterfly is one of six delicate animal studies by Per Lindstrom. Other designs are printed in stronger colors and, backed with firmer cotton, could be turned into centerpieces for pillows or quilts.

Sanderson-Kemp, a Scottish firm, made hand-printed "Pussie" herb-filled pillows and potpourri sachets, c.1975, for the gift trade. They were printed in either black or marmalade on white, and the general shape was based on the type of "sewn-up" fabric toy pioneered by the Arnold Print Works eighty years earlier.

Bed linen with cats is another possibility. Rows of Kliban cats wearing shoes tramp all over cotton sheets, and another Kliban cat, this time wearing a long red scarf, leaps across a bath towel. These items were bought in London, but made in the U.S.A. by Burlington Domestics. Beatrix Potter's cats have appeared on children's bedclothes and nursery curtains; more unusually, Randolph Caldecott's crouching cat has been printed on furnishing fabric together with other characters from his *House That Jack Built* illustrations.

Lesley Holmes's cats are familiar from greeting cards, but they have also appeared on textiles, including pillows and a selection of household items. In the 1970s Bruce Angrave's comic cats were well-known through his clever paper sculpture and his little books *CAT-alogue* and *Magnifi-CAT*; a blissfully sleeping Angrave tabby was turned into a cotton hot-water-bottle cover.

— 116 —

The artist Per Lindstrom designed this printed cotton handkerchief which shows a tabby cat. Made in Switzerland, it dates from c.1970.

— 117 —

Towel with a leaping Kliban cat is a marvelous item. It was made by Burlington Domestics in the U.S.

Some years ago, I was given what I can only suppose to be a table cover; it is obviously commercially produced, and I have seen identical examples, but the Victorian-style cats woven into the design seem strangely at odds with the Indian "feel" of the fabric, which appears to be a mixture of cotton and shiny rayon.

Rows of sitting cats form an eye-catching border for lace curtains from Nottingham, England. Nottingham lacemaking has a long history, and the crisp fabric retains its traditional look, even though manmade fibers are now often blended with cotton in the manufacturing process. These particular curtains were made by Basford Textiles, and I snapped them up as soon as I saw them in an open-air market.

In some cases it is difficult to decide whether an object is collectible or not – in other words, whether a type of cat exists in sufficient numbers for a collector to have a chance of finding one. This doubtful area includes all the home-made fabric cats that have found their way into thousands of charity bazaars – the knitted toys, appliqué felt oven gloves, potholders, laundry bags, and embroidered cases for handkerchiefs and nightgowns. Most collectors are only too pleased to be offered these humble survivors from a past age; recent textiles such as cat-printed T-shirts and intricate knitted sweaters will be the cat-bygones of tomorrow.

118

An American handmade sewing bag, 1920 or earlier, shows the Button Family on its four panels – Father, Mother, the Twins, and the Cat. Beside it stands an Austrian bronze thimble-holder in the form of a tailor cat with scissors and measuring tape, a 1984 reproduction by Heirloom Editions, U.S., of an original antique. The silver cat was made by English silversmith Kay Thetford Kendall.

GLASS
CATS

119

— 119 —

A cat with red glass
eyes reclines on the
lid of this covered
dish. Made of pressed
milk glass by
Atterbury of
Pittsburgh,
Pennsylvania, the dish
has a reticulated edge
and measures 6½in
× 8¼in.

This fluted oval covered dish, c.1880, shows a cat on a hamper. Made of pressed milk glass by McKee of Pittsburgh, Pennsylvania, it measures 4in × 5½in.

— 121 —

A 7-inch milk-glass plate, attributed to the Westmoreland Specialty Company, is designed to hang on the wall. The three kittens and the border are decorated with gold paint, and there is a gold ribbon for hanging.

his is another area in which European collectors envy their American friends, as it appears that glass cat dishes (or "cat-boxes") were produced only in the United States. Hen-on-nest dishes were certainly made in Europe, but glass cats sitting on basketweave bases seem to have been the specialty of a group of companies operating in Pennsylvania and West Virginia around the 1880s. The majority are of opaque white milk glass, but some were made in blue, black, or brown; the shape of the dish is either oval or rectangular, and the cat model reclines on the cover. Many consider that the finest dishes were made by the McKee Brothers of Pittsburgh, but the rarest and most sought-after dish was produced by the Atterbury Company, also of Pittsburgh; this rectangular dish has a lacy rim to the base and a cat with applied glass eyes; the design was patented in 1889.

121

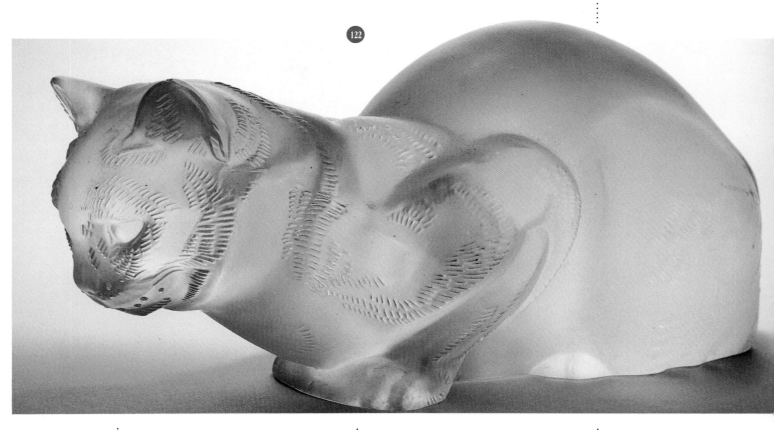

122

The Westmoreland Glass Company of Grapeville, Pennsylvania, made a "Three Kittens" plate in milk glass touched with gold paint, and showing a trio of kittens in relief overlapping the top one-third of the plate and a lacy border around the remainder; it would have been of no practical use and was obviously intended to be hung up as a decoration. Both this plate and several of the cat-covered dishes have been reproduced from old molds.

The French designer René Lalique produced some lovely crystal cats with the "iced" or frosted finish typical of his work. His best-known cat is in a crouching position with forelegs tucked under the chest. René Lalique died in 1945, but the Paris firm was carried on by his son Marc, and the famous crouching cat is still in production. Smaller Lalique cats popular with collectors are salt and pepper shakers with silver heads and frosted glass bodies.

Sabino of Paris also made cat figures in the 1920s. The same molds are still being used today, so it is still possible to buy modern Sabino cats.

It was interesting to see how many glass cats were on display in England at Salisbury Museum's Cat Exhibition held in 1991/2. Besides the Laliques, there was a superb French model in Baccarat crystal of a stylized sitting cat designed by R. Rigot. Another French model of a sitting cat, this time by Daum, was clearly influenced by representations of the Egyptian Bastet. A German cat by the Goebel firm was in frosted crystal on a clear plinth; other modern glass cats had come from Sweden, Portugal, Belgium, England, and Murano, in the Venetian lagoon.

Perfume bottles have been produced in cat shapes, especially popular in the Art Deco period of the 1930s. More recently, Avon cosmetics has marketed perfume in attractively designed cat bottles.

— —

A cat of frosted lead crystal by Lalique of Paris. Several elegant Lalique cats are still being made from the original molds and can be obtained from quality retailers.

123

A small French glass cat (left) : made by Sabino of opalescent glass, c.1920. The large cat on the right with its sassy black bow is an art deco perfume bottle, c.1930. The head forms the bottle stopper.

123

CHAPTER
NINE

CATS IN
ADVERTISING

— 124 —

A White Cat cigar box
label, American. Cats
have often been used
to promote tobacco
products.

The artist for this early 20th-century advertisement for Nestle's Milk was John Hassall. Cats were considered especially appropriate for promoting milk products.

dvertising and sales-promotion cats really form a major collecting category by themselves. Manufacturers of all sorts of goods have been quick to realize that the buying public takes notice of a striking cat illustration, somehow associating it with harmony, cleanliness, and other domestic virtues; and so cats are found recommending soap, metal polish, condensed milk, and a hundred other products. Before tobacco was frowned upon, they helped to sell cigars and cigarettes.

CHOCOLATE-BOX CATS
~

The cliché of the chocolate-box cat was coined in 1869 when Richard Cadbury of the famous confectionery firm hit upon the brilliant idea of adding a picture to the lid of an expensive box of chocolate creams. He painted the portrait of his daughter, "a blue-eyed maiden, some six summers old ... nursing a cat," to decorate the box, and the Cadbury's family pet became the first of a long line of winsome tabbies to act as powerful persuaders in the confectionery trade. Chocolate packaging is now usually disposable, but the more robust and luxurious boxes of the past were often kept long after the chocolates had gone, and used for storing buttons and other small objects; collectors could be lucky.

Well-made candy containers were especially popular in the United States, where cat-shaped receptacles with removable heads are eagerly collected. They can be dated back to c.1890 and were still being made in the 1930s, when the English firm of Sharps packed toffees into Giant Pandas, Teddy Bears, and Black Cats. Most of the containers were made of papier-mâché with a fabric covering, and the animals had glass eyes.

Printed tins form another collectible group; the most highly prized are the ornamental cookie tins issued by several firms for the Christmas trade. Huntley and Palmer's products were being packed in fancy tins by the 1870s, and for the next sixty years an amazing succession of fresh designs appeared every autumn. Tins were made to look like handbags, fishing creels, windmills, Moorish tables, baby buggies, and hundreds of even more unlikely objects. Many featured children and animals, including cats. One of Huntley and Palmer's most desirable late 19th-century boxes has its lid and sides covered with Wain-type cats and dogs playing tug-of-war at a Christmas party. "Pets" c.1890, from The Co-Operative Wholesale Society of Britain, has more cats and dogs, this time with children; "Puss," c.1909 from the same company is oval and ideally should still have its wool handles. Carr & Co. also issued a "Pets" tin c.1877, followed by "Juvenile No. 1 (Kittens)" in 1897 and "Little Romps," with a scene of kittens on the lid, in 1902.

— 126 —

A tape measure marked MADE IN U.S.A. has a celluloid case decorated with a cat picture.

The small black kitten on Mabel Lucie Attwell's "Bicky House" issued by William Crawford & Sons in 1933 plays only a supporting role in the design, but this miniature thatched cottage with a money-slot in its roof is so appealing that enthusiasts might count it as a cat-collectible. Many ornamental tins were designed to have a permanent function once the contents had been eaten; they became glove and stationery boxes or jewelry cases; others became toys – humming tops, buckets, and gypsy caravans among them.

Fancy boxes were an early casualty of World War II, and afterwards they became uneconomic to make. Very occasionally, candy and toffee are still packed in tins with pictorial lids: Blue Bird toffees, for example, were put into small tins printed with a group of kittens in the early 1960s, and in 1991 Bentley's of London packed fruit bonbons in oval tins bearing cat studies from *The Cats' Gallery of Art* by Susan Herbert.

Rarity and condition dictate the price of almost all collectibles, and connoisseurs will consider only items in near-mint condition. However, this leaves less-than-perfect specimens for buyers primarily interested in the feline content. Provided these items are acquired at the right price, and for pleasure and not for investment, they merit a place in a cat collection.

CAT ENDORSEMENT
~

Posters, press advertising, and printed packaging have innumerable cats to offer, and Louis Wain, Theophile-Alexandre Steinlen, and John Hassall are just three of the artists whose work is included in this field. Louis Wain drew cats for decorating boxes of Mazawattee Tea and for publicizing Millson's Baby Cars (here a bespectacled tabby pushes a kitten in a perambulator).

Steinlen's cats were much in demand by advertisers, and his great poster "Pure Sterilized Milk from the Vingeanne" has become a classic among collectors. Another of his remarkable cat posters, for the *Compagnie Française des Chocolats et des Thes* (c.1899) can be seen in New York's Metropolitan Museum and is splendidly reproduced in the Museum's book, *Metropolitan Cats*. John Hassall's conversational cats combine humor with a simple message singing the praises of Nestle's Milk in another vintage poster.

FOR CHRISTMAS
Shop between 10 & 4 *and travel*
UNDERGROUND

CATS ON TRADE CARDS

~

The cat was a favorite decorative motif on American advertising trade cards – thin cardboard, colorfully imprinted cards designed to advertise the merits of a product. Stock advertising trade cards were personalized by adding the name and address of a local merchant or distributor. Their appeal was universal. Adults and children alike collected and pasted them into albums. The golden age of the American trade card was 1880 to 1895, although examples dated as early as 1810 and as late as 1910 can be found.

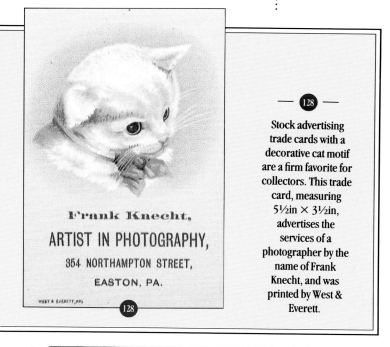

Frank Knecht,
ARTIST IN PHOTOGRAPHY,
354 NORTHAMPTON STREET,
EASTON, PA.

128

— 128 —

Stock advertising trade cards with a decorative cat motif are a firm favorite for collectors. This trade card, measuring 5½in × 3½in, advertises the services of a photographer by the name of Frank Knecht, and was printed by West & Everett.

Sewing thread from J. P. Coats had a lot of help from cats; in 1884 one of their advertisements showed a tethered bulldog frantically trying to reach a pair of cats; the cats, however, were in no danger as the dog is safely restrained by a single strand of Coats' thread. In another Coats' advertisement, four kittens – two striped tabbies, one black, and one white – are playing with a spool of thread while the message reads "White, Black and Colors for Hand & Machine." A miniature reproduction of this advertisement, incidentally,

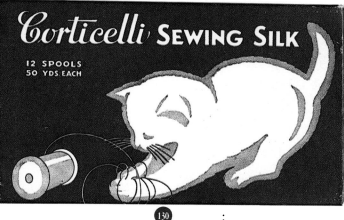

130

— 130 —

This is one of the many cats and kittens used to advertise Corticelli Sewing Silk. This playful white kitten entangled in the company's product decorates the lid of the cardboard box designed to hold twelve spools.

— 129 —

A late 19th-century advertisement for Coats Sewing Cotton is reproduced here in miniature on a matchbox by the Cornish Match Company.

has recently been used by the enterprising Cornish Match Company to decorate one of their nostalgic matchboxes in the "Great Grandfather's Day" series.

The Corticelli Silk Buttonhole Twist Company had a cat's head for its trademark, while cooking oil, pianos, tobacco, and rye whiskey were among other products to be promoted by cats in early U.S. advertisements. In England the best-known feline in the publicity world is probably the striking Black Cat of the old Carreras Tobacco posters. The firm's palatial headquarters in north London had giant black cat

129

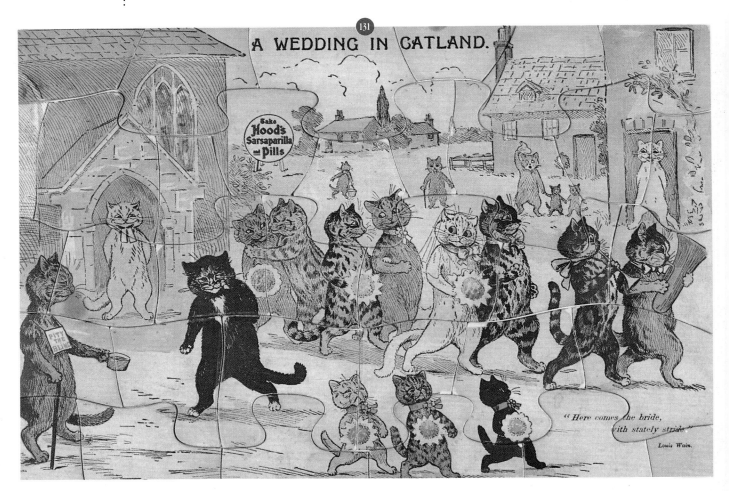

A WEDDING IN CATLAND.

"Here comes the bride, with stately stride."

Louis Wain.

statues guarding the front doors, while the familiar face could be seen everywhere gazing out from large enamel signs. Few people could have foreseen, in the 1930s, that these signs would become prized as collectors' items, and hundreds – probably thousands – of them must have been thrown away when old buildings were pulled down after World War II. The one in my own collection came to light when I put my foot through the floor of a tumbledown garden shed and discovered that some previous occupant had tried to reinforce the boards by sliding the sheet-metal sign underneath them.

Pears Soap advertisements have great charm, and at the turn of the century, the British company invested heavily in publicity, not only through the press, but also in an entertaining and lavishly illustrated "annual." With this magazine came free color prints suitable for framing; one which includes kittens is "The Invaders" by the prolific Edwardian artist Arthur Elsley.

"Globe" Metal Polish was vigorously sponsored by assorted cats, usually wearing placards around their necks wittily advising shoppers to "Ask for the Globe Polish, and see that you get it!" Robert Opie's wonderful collection at the Museum of Advertising and Packaging in Gloucester, England, has several Globe cats cut from cardboard which were intended for counter displays.

The use of a point-of-purchase or proof-of-purchase premium as an inducement to buy a product was well established by the turn of the

— 131 —

A prized piece for a collector is this advertising jigsaw puzzle "A wedding in Catland and Hood's Bridge Puzzle," which was manufactured by C.I. Hood Co., Lowell, Massachusetts. It is 14½in × 9⅞in.

"CHESSIE"
~

"Chessie" was the well-loved mascot of the Chesapeake and Ohio Railroad. The sleepy tabby, designed by the Viennese artist Guido Gruenwald, promised travelers a good night's rest as they sped across America in the railroad's sleeping cars in the 1930s and '40s. "Peake," another engaging tabby, was "Chessie's" companion. These two cat images were skillfully converted into needlepoint by Erica Wilson.

132

— 132 —

A 1957 calendar issued by the Chesapeake & Ohio Railway uses a sleeping Chessie the Kitten to convey the reassuring idea that passengers traveling on this railroad would enjoy a good night's rest.

twentieth century. A prized piece on both sides of the Atlantic is the C. I. Hood Company's doubled-sided advertising jigsaw puzzle entitled "A Wedding in Catland and Hood's Bridge Puzzle." Louis Wain did the wedding illustration for the Lowell, Massachusetts, firm. Die-cut examples bring premium prices. Souvenir pieces also doubled as advertising in many cases. Tix, the celebrated Angora Cat of Green's Hotel, Philadelphia, graces a giveaway paperweight.

Edward Bawden, one of Britain's most original and versatile 20th-century artists, designed the covers for Fortnum and Mason's Christmas catalogs in 1956 and 1958; for 1958 he drew cats in immaculate evening dress sitting around a dinner table and, in the foreground, a large tabby wearing a Santa Claus outfit complete with false beard. Thousands of these catalogs must have been sent out to Fortnum & Mason's customers, and there is always a chance of coming across one that was put away.

— 133 —

The front cover of the 1958 Christmas catalog issued by Fortnum & Mason of London shows a cat Santa Claus complete with beard and whiskers. The artist was the highly versatile Edward Bawden. (By kind permission of Fortnum & Mason.)

— 134 —

Measuring 29in wide and 35½in high, this paper kite of Morris the Cat advertising 9-lives Cat Food was a sure seller.

"Hirondelle" wine was advertised in 1977 with a clever illustration by Peter le Vasseur showing a crowd of cheerful cats and dogs falling out of a blue sky; the caption reads, predictably enough, "It's about as likely as a duff bottle of Hirondelle." Well-printed on good quality paper, the advertisement appeared in the Christmas Number of *Country Life* magazine in December 1977. In fact, it is worthwhile leafing through copies of old magazines to have a look at the glossy advertising.

In England, cutout figures of a fluffy white cat used to be seen in showrooms displaying "Kosset" carpets. Another white cat, the famous Arthur, helped to sell Katto-meat pet food by appearing on television and scooping the food out of a tin with his left paw; he then ate it with evident relish. Arthur made over thirty commercials between 1966 and 1975, and after he died the

following year (aged almost seventeen), he was replaced by Arthur II, once an inmate of an animal sanctuary. In the U.S. a cat named Morris had a similar acting career, endorsing 9-Lives cat food and winning a "best animal actor" award in 1973. He was succeeded by Morris II, found in a cats' home, who went on to become as famous as his predecessor. Arthur I and Morris I both had their biographies published, and collectors of cat books should look out for them.

For Christmas 1988, British retailer Marks and Spencer packed its own-brand cat food in a cardboard container made to represent a small one-story building being used as a Cats' Pantry: it is unusual to find pet food in such imaginative packaging; but when it does appear, collectors with an eye to the future will appreciate its potential as one of tomorrow's curiosities.

KITCHEN CATS

— 135 —

A Japanese ceramic
teapot in the form of
a cat. The tail serves
as the handle, while
the beverage is
poured out through
the captive goldfish's
mouth. (Faith Eaton
Collection).

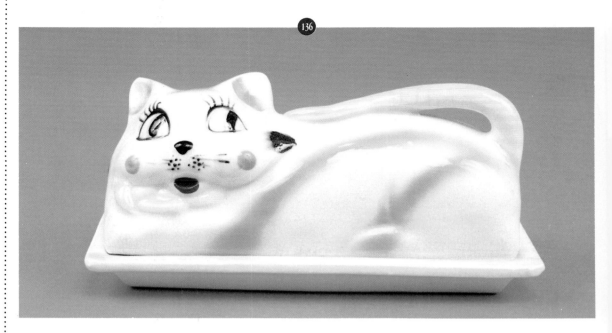

This eye-catching ceramic butterdish has no. 52/724 stamped on the bottom and measures 6½in by 3in.

Kitchen cats are ideal for anyone not wanting to take collecting too seriously, or to spend a lot of money. Cat motifs have been used to decorate almost every item of modern kitchen paraphernalia, with mugs, trays, toaster covers, storage jars, and teapots just a few of the dozens of cat-related objects for sale in any ordinary general store.

The connection between cozy felines and kitchen equipment can be traced back to a period much earlier than the age of the ubiquitous printed dishcloth. Wooden gingerbread molds in cat shapes were certainly known in the 18th century – Brighton Museum, England, has a splendid one – and today dealers trade in "kitchenalia," with fluctuating supplies of cat-decorated china, ice-cream molds, and string holders dating back to the early years of this century and before. Writing in the 1880s, Harrison Weir recalled seeing Puss-in-Boots gingerbread being sold at fairs, as well as "cats made of cheese, sweet sponge cake, sugar" and, once, a cat made of gelatin.

Molds representing cats are now widely available in rigid plastic, though the gelatin product is a somewhat flat, spreading animal. More artistic results come from using small tin chocolate molds, or cookie or pastry cutters.

It would be an interesting exercise to set up a practical, modern kitchen with equipment illustrating the cat drawings of contemporary artists. Lesley Anne Ivory, for example, celebrated worldwide for her amazingly realistic cats and detailed backgrounds, has seen her pets put on

This two-part zinc candy mold showing three cats was made by T. Mills of Philadelphia, Pennsylvania, between 1900 and 1925. It measures 1in × 1¼in.

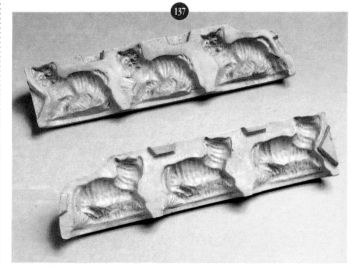

138

A modern mass-produced square tin tray from 1992 carries a Lesley Anne Ivory cat design surrounded by a floral border.

— 139 —

A rectangular blue and white kettle holder was handcrafted on Martha's Vineyard Island by Woodchips Designers in the U.S. in the 1980s.

mats, trays, towels, storage jars, and tea cozies, transforming a host of everyday objects into collectors' items. A set of twelve plates showing her family's own kittens was issued by Danbury Mint in 1990 under the title "Meet My Kittens." Appealing to both cat-lovers and plate collectors, they were not intended for normal use, but would make a wonderful display on a kitchen shelf.

Lesley Holmes is another artist known for her cats. Her distinctive models gaze out from mugs, aprons,

tea cozies, shopping bags, and an ever-growing assortment of household accesories. Sue Boettcher's cats, sleek and black, look good on plain white bone china mugs and various sizes of tin container.

Designs for cat-inspired linen dishcloths must run into hundreds, if not thousands, and even the keenest collector in this field has to be selective. Besides being put to their primary use, towels can be hung up like posters or framed, or turned into tray cloths or curtains for a small kitchen window.

Mugs, too, come in their thousands, ranging from very cheap to surprisingly expensive. Mugs with a cat connection can be hung from low beams as part of a decorative scheme. There is a wide choice of cartoon and comic character cats – the Kliban animal, for example, and Garfield – as well as innumerable conventional portraits of every type from smooth to fluffy.

— 140 —

A mug and two 10-inch plates are from a set of six issued by the British National Trust. The designs, taken from some hand-painted plates displayed in the kitchen of the Trust's property, at Kingston Lacy, date from 1880. The dishes were originally used by children of the then owners, the Bankes family.

— 141 —

Garfield glass mugs, 3⅛in × 3½in. Copyright attributed to United Feature Syndicate Inc.

THE OWL AND THE PUSSY-CAT WENT TO SEA
IN A BEAUTIFUL PEA-GREEN BOAT,
THEY TOOK SOME HONEY, AND PLENTY OF MONEY,
WRAPPED UP IN A FIVE-POUND NOTE.
THE OWL LOOKED UP TO THE STARS ABOVE.
AND SANG TO A SMALL GUITAR
'O LOVELY PUSSY! O PUSSY, MY LOVE,
WHAT A BEAUTIFUL PUSSY YOU ARE.
YOU ARE,
YOU ARE!'
WHAT A BEAUTIFUL PUSSY
YOU ARE!

A set of six hand-painted plates, each showing a different cat and dating from about 1888, is displayed in the kitchen of the British National Trust's house at Kingston Lacy, where they were originally used by children of the Banks family. The Trust produces sets of plates and mugs inspired by these covetable and unusual pieces; being blue and white, they fit in well with any traditional kitchen decoration, and many collectors will want to add at least one or two of the plates to their display shelves. A linen dishcloth reproducing five of the cat designs is also available. My advice is to buy such items on sight.

Another semi-exclusive piece of kitchenware comes from the shop at London's Royal Academy of Arts: this is a delightful enamel bowl, soup-plate size, printed in black with Edward Lear's drawing of the Owl and the Pussy Cat and bordered with other Lear animal curiosities, including his own lovable Foss. Supplies are spasmodic, so buy when you can.

A 10-inch enamel bowl is printed with drawings by Edward Lear and carries a verse from his poem, *The Owl and the Pussycat*. Produced by Mikkimugs of England, it was a souvenir produced for a Lear exhibition at the Royal Academy of Art in London and bought c.1988.

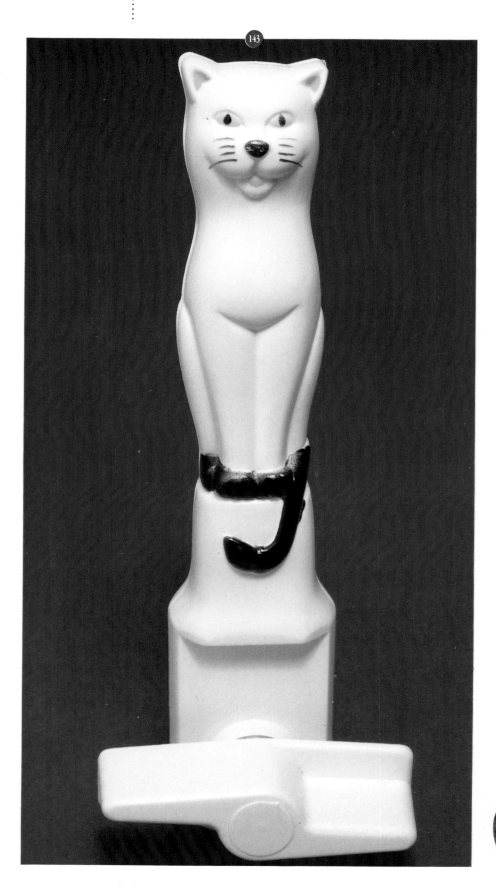

Boxes for holding a ball of string, traditionally made of brass or cast iron, can also be found in chalkware and ceramics. In an American chalkware version of about 1900, a striped cat holds a spherical ball of yarn, with the real ball of twine fitting inside the chalkware one. The English version has a hollow cat's head in earthenware to hold the string, with the end threaded through the mouth and a useful pair of scissors tucked into the neck ribbon. Both pieces are designed to hang on a wall. The latest English string-carrying cats have a well-modeled natural shape and come in an assortment of ginger and bicolor markings; made at the Babbacombe Pottery, they would make an amusing and useful addition to a kitchen.

An even more practical item with a feline theme is a special can opener. Recommended as being hygienic, the gadget has strong molded plastic handles representing a white cat; it comes from Hong Kong, with a companion piece for dog-food. Almost any shop selling cheap gifts and souvenirs will display an astonishing array of other items for the

143

This modern can opener has a stately white cat as its handle and comes from Hong Kong.

144

Two ceramic stringholders, for hanging on the wall. The ball of twine fits inside the head and the end is threaded through the mouth, the top one is unmarked and the one below is English made by Babbacombe pottery.

145

The white cat climbing up the side of this ceramic mustard pot forms its handle. Complete with lid and spoon, it is typical of many pots and pitchers made in Germany in the late 19th century.

145

— **146** —

This Halloween wooden refrigerator magnet is hand-painted and 2⅜in high.

cat-lover's kitchen; Fridge Magnets for attaching reminder notes to the refrigerator door are mostly imported from the Far East and include cats of every known breed. Egg-timers worked by falling sand are still made, often attached to a plaster ornament incorporating a lucky black cat; these have been popular souvenirs for generations. There are cat chopping boards and racks to hold mugs or household keys, ceramic wall tiles, and even flying cats (instead of 1930s ducks) to add a bizarre touch.

Finally, there are things for a cat-lover's cat: a choice of attractive feeding bowls, and some suitable plastic mats to stand them on would add to the overall effect at little expense.

— **147** —

A pair of salt and pepper shakers from Shawnee, 3³⁄₁₆in high, entitled "Puss'n'Boots," were designed by Rudy Ganz. They are American; the design dates from the 1940s and 50s.

CHARACTER CATS

148

— 148 —

An amusing Sylvester
hot water bottle from
Warner Bros. Inc.,
made in Spain. It
measures 12¾in
high.

Comic strips, movie cartoons, Saturday morning television cartoons, and feature-length movies have produced a group of cat characters beloved by young and old alike. Many of these inanimate felines are so real in our minds that we talk about them as though they are human. Many are recognized internationally, e.g., Felix and Garfield. Others enjoy more limited recognition, e.g. Ooloo and Heathcliff.

Not all are heroes. In fact, many have earned their claim to fame by portraying classic villains. Sylvester's pursuit of Tweety Pie, Mighty Mouse's conquests of Oil Can Harry and Sourpuss, and Tom's continual, but futile attempts to catch Jerry have evoked laughter for over half a century. Despite being crushed, mauled, trampled, and subjected to a host of never ending abuses on a regular basis, these villainous cats exhibit a determined tenacity that has earned them grudging admiration even from their harshest critics.

Several of these character cats have celebrated their fiftieth birthday. In order to keep them fresh, their appearance is continually altered and updated. A 1990 Felix is very different from a 1920s Felix.

Several collectors have assembled collections focusing solely on the evolution of a single character cat.

Most of these character cats make multiple appearances. Felix, who began as a movie cartoon cat, also starred in a comic strip, comic book series, and several books. Garfield, a comic strip cat, is featured in a number of prime-time television specials as well as serving as an advertising spokesperson in print and on television.

The enormous popularity of character cats can be seen in the wide range of character cat collectibles they have generated. There is virtually no collecting category, from ceramics to toys, that has not been

— 149 —

Felix the Cat souvenir for the bathroom, measuring 10¼in high and made by Colgate-Palmolive Co.

— 150 —

Felix the Cat stuffed, walking toy; this is one of the many models of this popular feline made in the 1920s and '30s. (Faith Eaton Collection.)

151

Homemade walker
toy of Felix the Cat.
Made of wood it
measures 18⅞in
high when standing
up straight.

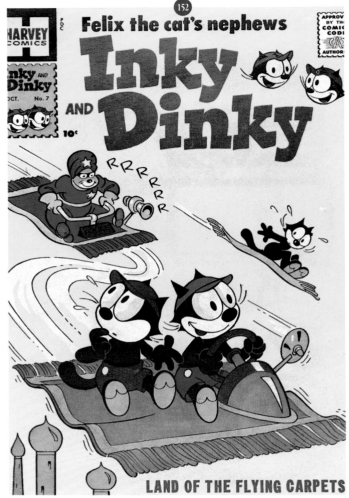

Felix the cat's nephews

Inky AND **Dinky**

HARVEY COMICS

Inky AND Dinky

OCT. No. 7

10¢

RRRRRR

LAND OF THE FLYING CARPETS

— 152 —

Colorful comic book containing Felix the Cat's adventures; this one titled "Land of the Flying Carpets," featuring Felix's nephews, Inky & Dinky, dated October 1958. Published by Harvey Comics.

touched. A detailed list would require a volume in itself.

Since the focus of this book is the domesticated cat, this chapter must limit itself to those character cats who live within a domestic environment. The Pink Panther and Cool Cat (a tiger) are not at home here. What follows is a character cat hall of fame. Enjoy.

MOVIE (ANIMATED) CARTOON CATS
~

FELIX

Felix is the most famous animated cartoon cat, a hero of the silent as well as talking screen. While Felix's exact origins are in dispute, it is safe

to say that Felix evolved through the combined efforts of Australian-born film-maker Pat Sullivan and artist Otto Messmer. Felix starred in over eighty short cartoons in the 1920s. During the height of the 1920s Felix craze, the song *Felix Kept on Walking* was sung everywhere. A host of Felix-inspired collectibles followed.

In 1923 Felix first appeared in a Sunday comic strip, followed in 1927 by a daily strip. The strip continues today under the auspices of Joe Oriolo Productions. In 1930 when NBC selected the first cartoon for television broadcast, the choice was simple – FELIX.

Alienated, but obstinate, Felix is a fighter. His adventures took him to a number of exotic places ranging from outer space to dream worlds. The love of his life was the flighty Phyllis. Most remember Felix as walking back and forth with his hands behind his back "thinking" through problems.

PERCY

Percy, a villainous cat, who was in constant pursuit of Little Roquefort, a witty and troublesome mouse, appeared regularly on the CBS television network "The Heckle and

 — 153 —

This 11in × 8½in Percy Puss frame tray jigsaw puzzle is published by Terrytoons Inc., E. E. Fairchild Corp., Rochester, New York.

LITTLE ROQUEFORT AND PERCY PUSS

153

The infamous "I taut I saw a Puddy-Tat" sheet music with words and music by Alan Livingstone & Billy May, published by Remic Music Corp., New York and Printed by Lowe & Brydone Printers Ltd., London.

Jeckle Show" which aired in the late 1950s through the 1960s. Percy was built on the success of Terrytoons Mighty Mouse, a tireless fighter against Oil Can Harry and Sourpùss. Alas for poor Percy, the real star was Little Roquefort. Percy collectibles are difficult to find.

SYLVESTER

Sylvester made his first, albeit un-named appearance, in "A Tale of Two Kitties," a 1942 Bob Clampett animated cartoon. Named by Friz Freleng, an animation director, Sylvester, a black cat with white markings, spends much of his life unsuccessfully chasing a canary named Tweety Pie. Sylvester made guest appearances in many Warner Brothers cartoons, ranging from *The Bugs Bunny Show* to *The Porky Pig Show*. It was Mel Blanc's unique voice that created one of the best known cartoon phrases – "Sufferin' succotash!"

TOM

Joseph Barbera and William Hanna created the characters of Tom and Jerry in 1939 while under contract to MGM. The cartoons follow a basic

155

Tom, from Tom and Jerry fame, depicted on a hot water bottle. It is 12in high and was made in Spain.

theme – Jerry, a small mouse, makes Tom, a large cat, angry, the result of which is a chase scene heavy in choreographed violence. In the late 1950s and early 1960s Gene Deitch of Terrytoons produced a second series of Tom and Jerry cartoons for MGM in Prague. A third series was produced by Chuck Jones for Warner Brothers. Tom and Jerry appeared on American television from September 1965 to September 1972. In 1976 Hanna and Barbera created a new set of TV cartoons. Tom and Jerry appear on a wide range of collectibles from comic books to jigsaw puzzles.

COMIC-STRIP CATS
~

FRITZ THE CAT
Robert Crumb, underground illustrator, created Fritz the Cat in 1959, beginning as a youthful optimist and ending as a selfish cynic. The strip called attention to the social changes of the turbulent 1960s. The strip was violent and crude, appealing to college students with a call to "tune in, turn on, and drop out." Fritz appeared in comic form in 1968, book form in 1969, and as an animated cartoon in 1970, the first cartoon to receive an "X" rating. Fritz died in 1972.

KRAZY KAT

George Herriman's Krazy Kat originally appeared in 1910 as a substrip of "The Dingbat Family," gaining his own strip in October 1913. Krazy Kat, a resident of Coconimo Country, produced social satire focusing on identity, the nature of personal relationships, and societal structure. This undefined secular black cat showed traits of empathy, generosity, gentleness, and optimism. The cartoon strip ended with Herriman's death in 1944. A number of animated cartoons, a ballet, and a novel, Gilbert Seldes' *The Seven Lively Arts,* glorified Krazy Kat.

OOLOO

George Studdy, a well-known English cartoonist best remembered as creator of the dog Bonzo, invented a

— 157 —

These hard-to-find Pez containers showing Arlene, Nermal and Garfield were made in Austria and are each 4in high.

157

— 156 —

A pinback button depicting Fritz the Cat. Fritz the Cat comic strip was the first to receive an "X" rating.

GARFIELD

Jim Davis created Garfield on June 19, 1978, for United Feature Syndicate. In 1987 the strip appeared in 2,000 plus newspapers. Avoiding any social or political comment, Garfield is a cynical, fat, lazy cat whose principal role in life is to entertain. The butt of many of Garfield's jokes is Odie, the dog. Garfield is everywhere – a Saturday morning animated cartoon show, numerous television specials, books, plays, costumed personal appearances, and as a spokesperson for products ranging from Alpo to McDonalds. There are over 6,000 licensed Garfield collectibles.

HEATHCLIFF

George Gately created Heathcliff on September 3, 1973, for the McNaught Syndicate. Heathcliff a crafty, smug, fat, striped cat is known for getting what he wants, dominating all with whom he comes into contact. Heathcliff's children's animated cartoon series features the voice of Mel Blanc.

mischievous cat called Ooloo, whose comic strip adventures began in early 1929. Like Bonzo, Ooloo was quickly turned into a toy (already on sale in three sizes for Christmas 1929). Many collectors have a black velvet cat with pink face and paws in their collection without being aware of its true identity.

SATURDAY-MORNING TELEVISION CATS
~

KLONDIKE KAT
Klondike Kat was part of the CBC animated cartoon series "King Leonardo and His Short Subjects" (1960–61) and "Tennessee Tuxedo and His Tales" (1963–66). Like most Saturday morning television cat tales, this show featured the traditional cat versus mouse story. Klondike Kat, a member of the Klondike Cops, patrolled the mining camps of the American west. His antogonist was a mouse thief called Savoir Fare, known for his love of gourmet food.

MR. JINKS
Mr. Jinks, a cantakerous cat, along with his nemeses, the two mice Pixie and Dixie, appeared as part of Hanna-Barbera's "The Huckleberry Hound Show." Mr. Jinks' key identification is a polka dot bowtie and the phrase "I hate you 'meeses' to pieces!" Mr. Jinks' television career lasted from 1958 to 1962.

PUNKIN' PUSS
Punkin' Puss and Mush Mouse was a segment of the "Magilla Gorilla Show" which aired on ABC between January 1966 and December 1967. Hanna-Barbera chose a hillbilly theme for this cartoon. As friends and antagonists, Punkin' Puss and Mush Mouse survived the hardships ·and perils of rural mountain life.

158

159

A bright Mr. Jinks bubble bath bottle accompanied by Pixie and Dixie, 10in high, and produced by Barbera Productions Inc., Purex Corp Ltd.

— 159 —

Punkin Puss and Mush Mouse Bubble Club Bath Bottles. Produced by Hanna Barbera Productions, Inc., Purex Corp. Ltd.

RIFF RAFF

Riff Raff and the Junkyard Cats air as a segment of "Heathcliff," an afternoon children's cartoon show on the cable Nickleodeon channel. Riff Raff is a brown, scruffy, thin cat who lives with his gang in a junkyard. The love of his life is Cleo.

RUFF

Joseph Barbera and William Hanna created Ruff, a small, quick-thinking cat, and Reddy, a lovable, but not so intelligent dog, animated cartoon series in December 1957. It was Hanna-Barbera's first successful television series, last aired in September 1964.

— 160 —

Little Golden Book with the title *Ruff and Reddy* by Ann McGovern, published by Golden Press, New York, 1959.

TOP CAT

Hanna-Barbera based Top Cat, a master con artist, on Phil Silvers' Sergeant Bilko character from "The Phil Silvers Show." The show aired on ABC (September 1961 to March 1963) and NBC (April 1965 to December 1966). Top Cat, known as "T.C.," was the leader of a pack of Broadway alley cats who exhibit anti-social behavior. The theme of the cartoons was a carefree life among the trash cans, occasionally interrupted by police officer Dibble, who never could quite catch the elusive Broadway gang.

MOVIE CATS
~

Cartoon and television character cats are responsible for over ninety-nine percent of character cat collectibles. However, this chapter would not be complete without mentioning a few of the great movie cats. In the full length animated cartoon field, Disney

Studios/Buena Vista is responsible for Figaro from *Pinocchio;* the Cheshire Cat from *Alice in Wonderland,* and *The Aristocats.* Cat actors have earned their stripes in films such as *Bell, Book and Candle* (1958), featuring Pyewacket, *Harry and Tonto* (1974), a cross-country epic of a man and his cat, *Rhubarb* (1951) about a cat who inherits a baseball team, and *That Darn Cat* (Walt Disney Buena/Vista, 1965) featuring D.C., a silvery Siamese. The list could easily be expanded to include hundreds of films in which cats made cameo and supporting appearances.

Movie cat character collectibles are difficult to find. The prime source are lobby cards, movie posters, press books, and publicity stills. Books and scripts from plays upon which many of the movies are based help build a collection. Don't give up. Movie cat character collectibles do exist.

— 161 —

Top Cat: leader of the rebellious Broadway gang, created by Hanna-Barbera. It stands 10⅛in high.

CHAPTER
TWELVE

VARIOUS
CATS

— 162 —

This photograph is used on publicity material for the delightful Museum of Miniature Furniture at the Chateau de Vendeuvre, Saint-Pierre-sur-Dives in Normandy, France.

Museums are good places to find unusual cats. In London both the Victoria and Albert and the British Museum have published books on the cats in their collections, and New York's Metropolitan Museum has produced a splendid volume devoted to its cat paintings, drawings, and prints. Replicas of Egyptian goddess cats and of a Roman model in blue ceramic are sold at the British Museum, and the Metropolitan Museum shop recently had paper napkins printed with cats from the paintings there for sale.

In Switzerland there is a private Cat Museum in Riehen, just outside Basel. Its 10,000 exhibits were assembled by two cat-lovers and include toys, porcelain, faience, fabrics, pictures, postage stamps, and postcards.

Although the Gallery of Naive Art in Bath, England, does not specialize in cats, it does have a successful print of a pair of 19th-century cats for sale. Like many other galleries (the Tate in London is especially good), it sells postcards of its cats.

There are also occasional temporary exhibitions with informative catalogs and posters destined to become collectors' items. In 1972 the Louis Wain celebration at London's Victoria and Albert Museum was accompanied by an excellent catalog and a bright pink poster featuring a tennis-playing cat. In 1990 Newcastle-upon-Tyne Art Gallery had an exhibition of paintings by the British Victorian artist Ralph Hedley, with a poster showing his popular tabby *Blinking in the Sun* (1881). In Paris, a four-day Cat Show in 1898 was publicized by a large colored poster, while in 1981 a trio of cats by the naive painter Duranton carried on the poster tradition.

Ceramic tiles decorated with cats have a long and distinguished history stretching back to Dutch Delft wares of the 17th century. Birmingham

— 163 —

This replica of an Egyptian blue-glazed ceramic cat from the Roman period, 1st century is one of several excellent pieces produced for the British Museum, which also sells models of bronze Bastet cats.

163

This colorful poster was issued by London's Victoria and Albert Museum to announce a major Louis Wain exhibition in 1973. The catalog for the show, in a bright purple cover, is another item much sought by collectors.

(England) Museum has a six-tile panel by the late-Victorian designer William de Morgan, showing two tabbies and a wicker cat basket. Now that tiles are again fashionable in kitchens and bathrooms, specialist shops are offering a good selection of modern cat tiles, some based on traditional blue-and-white designs and others with colorful up-to-the-minute animals.

Wallpaper cats, too, can be traced back at least to the 19th century: a fluffy Persian on a French paper of

CATS IN JEWELRY
~

Many pieces of jewelry have been inspired by cats. Although the dazzling creatures favored by the Duchess of Windsor were majestic jungle beasts, ordinary household pets have been portrayed on brooches and earrings: a little Victorian cat-in-shoe silver brooch was evidently based on some favorite illustration, as it appears again on a Christmas card of the same period. There were Art Deco brooches in the 1930s, and later jewelry made effective use of colored plastics. Ceramic brooches and earrings are currently being produced in Mexico and finding their way into craft stores. Miniature cats carved from jade are exported from Thailand, and although they cannot actually be worn, they have a certain jewel-like quality.

165

A black and white cat sits inside a larger black plastic cat brooch. Made by Amiee Bananee in 1989, it was bought the same year in California.

166
A Scottish "Sans Peur" silver cat badge that is hallmarked.

167
This large, flashy rhinestone, brooch shows a seated cat with black eyes and a huge bow around its neck. It was bought in 1990 from a street trader in London.

168
This enamel brooch, c.1930, shows three cats, each a different color and wearing a neck bow, sitting under a lamp post.

169
Silver cat brooch made in Peru by G. Iaffi, bought in London in 1980.

170
An angular French silvered metal Art Deco cat brooch, c.1930.

171
A silver English-made brooch showing a cat in front of an open fire with two cat ornaments on the mantlepiece, made by Philip (Pip) Isern of Methwold near Thetford, Norfolk, England, c.1987.

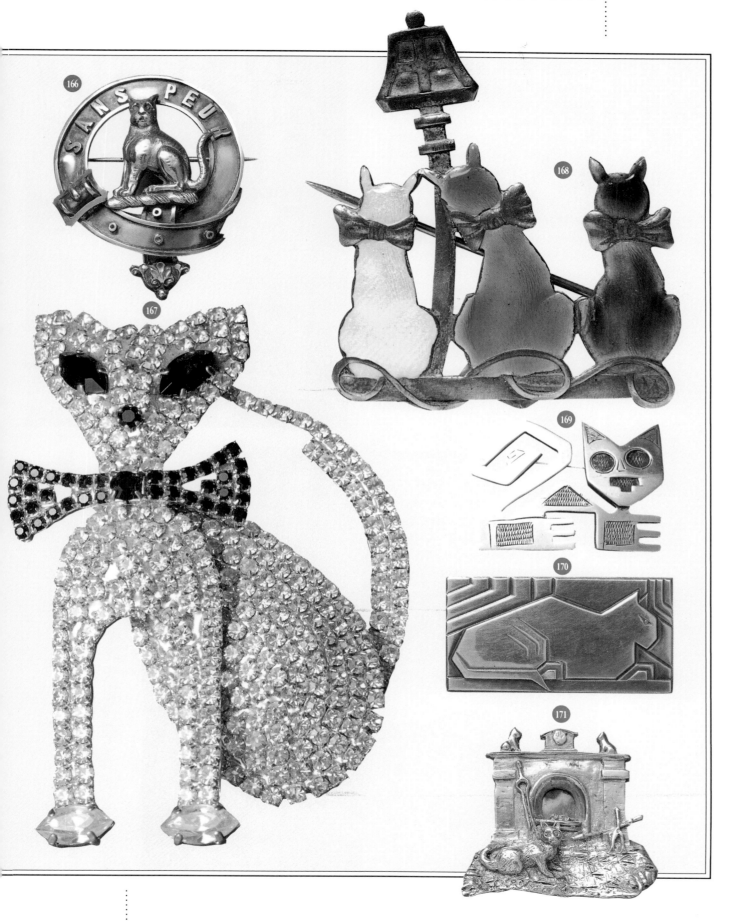

c.1830, and versatile Walter Crane-designed nursery wallpapers in the 1870s, one using his Cat-and-Fiddle illustration and another showing a strange medieval-looking cat on a squared tile pattern. Neither has been reproduced, but samples of the originals are safely stored in official archive collections. Meanwhile modern wallpaper friezes with cats are being produced by Designers' Guild (*Pussy-Cat, Pussy-Cat*) and Laura Ashley (*Hey-Diddle-Diddle*).

Cats on matchboxes are another specialist field with its own knowledgeable enthusiasts. On a completely different scale, there are cats as garden ornaments and as decorations for roof ridges, and climbing cats to attach to exterior walls.

The howling of a cat is music to a cat lover's ears. The singing nature of cats made them an ideal candidate for inclusion in the cover art of sheet music, records, pantomime and theatrical programs. A sheet music collection is a visual delight. The same song often appears with a variety of covers. Collectors vie to obtain both American, English, and Continental examples of the same tune. A music sheet cover featuring a

design by a famous illustrator, such as America's Grace Drayton, triples and often quadruples the value. Record jackets are a double delight when the song inside is about a cat. Theatrical programs featuring cats often reflect the finest artistic design of their period. Finally, do not forget

— —

Sheet music for "Kitten on the Keys," with lyrics by Sam Coslow, music by Zez Confrey, and published by Jack Mills Inc., New York.

— 172 —

This cat-shaped soap lies curled in a wicker basket on a gingham pillow. It is English and dates from the 1980s.

the music box. An American series features the cat designs of Lesley Anne Ivory.

Wax cat-candles present a problem; if they are attractive, it seems a pity to light them; some have a lovely finish comparable with the complexions of vintage wax dolls and cost as much as a ceramic model. There is in fact a kitten-in-boot mold currently being used to turn out candles, bronze-type cold castings, and small cement garden ornaments: further proof, if proof were needed, of the cat's popularity in any medium.

Sewing and mending are necessary household chores, a product of domesticity. As a means of entertaining the seamstress and adding attractiveness to their products, manufacturers of sewing implements often used a cat as the decorative motif. Cats can be found everywhere, from pincushions to measuring tapes. A souvenir silver thimble from Salem, Massachusetts, featured a black cat. The extreme popularity of the Corticelli cat and use of cats on the advertising trade cards of the J. P. Coats thread company was shown earlier in the Advertising and Packaging chapter.

While nobody would claim that all cat-related items available in the late 20th century are destined to be the antiques of tomorrow, many of them are charming and amusing, and they add interest and variety to a more serious collection. A cat-shaped rubber hot-water bottle, for example, bought in a London market in the 1970s, is probably a rarity already. A Chinese paper fan costing only pennies, a ceramic cat made in the U.S.S.R., a pair of bedroom slippers, a selection of key rings, cat-decorated sunglasses, and a yo-yo toy were all bought on impulse; and all, in their own way, are worthy of a place in any collection.

— 174 —

These contemporary, porcelain thimbles with a cat motif are hand-painted and stand 1¼in high.

— 175 —

This rubber hot water bottle is quite comic. It was bought in a London street market in the 1970s. The maker and origin are unknown.

BIBLIOGRAPHY

Artley, Alexandra. *The Great All-Picture CAT SHOW*. London: Astragal Books: 1977.

Ash, Russell (ed.). *Dear Cats: The Post Office Letters*. London: Pavilion Books Ltd.: 1986.

Blackbeard, Bill and Malcolm Whyte. *Great Comic Cats*. San Francisco: Troubador Press: 1981.

Bruce, Erika. *The Great Cat Game Book*. London: Michael Joseph: 1985.

Canemaker, John. *Felix, The Twisted Tale of the World's Most Famous Cat*. New York: Pantheon Books: 1991.

Clutton-Brock, Juliet. *The British Museum Book of Cats*. London: British Museum Publications Ltd.: 1988.

Dale, Rodney. *LOUIS WAIN: The Man Who Drew Cats*. London: Michael O'Mara Books Ltd.: 1968 and 1991.

deLys, Claudia and Frances Rhudy. *Centuries of Cats*. Connecticut: Silvermine Publishers, Inc.: 1971.

Dixon, Thomas W., Jr. *CHESSIE, The Railroad Kitten*. Virginia: TLC Publishing Company: 1988.

Fish, Enrica. *The Cat in Art*. Minnesota: Lerner Publishing Company: 1970.

Flick, Pauline. *Christmas Cats*. London: Collins: 1981.

Hart, Cynthia, John Grossman, and Josephine Banks. *Parlor Cats*. New York: Workman Publishing: 1991.

Hoffmann, Werner. *Katzen*. München: Wilhelm Heyne Verlag: 1980. Printed in German.

Horay, Pierre (ed.). *Cartespostales de Chats*. Paris: Horay Publications: 1984. Printed in French.

Johnson, Bruce. *American Cat-alogue*. New York: Avon Books: 1976.

Johnson, Peter. *Cats and Dogs, Phillips Collectors Guide*. London: Dunestyle Publishing Ltd. and Boxtree Ltd.: 1988.

Klever, Ulrich. *Knaurs Grosses Katzenbuch*. München: Droemer Knaur Verlag: 1985.

Lynnlee, J. L. *Purrrfection: The Cat*. Pennsylvania: Schiffer Publishing Ltd.: 1990.

McClinton, Katharine Morrison. *Antique Cats for Collectors*. Guildford and London: Lutterworth Press: 1974.

Maery, Fernand. *The Life, History and Magic of THE CAT*. New York: Grosset & Dunlap Publishing: 1968. Translated by Emma Street.

Müller, Rosemarie. *Katzen Museum: Mystik und Poesie*. Stuttgart, Germany: A. T.

Verlag: 1987. Printed in German.

Muncaster, Alice L., and Ellen Yanow. *The Cat Made Me Buy It!* New York: Crown Publishers, Inc.: 1984.

—, *The Cat Sold It!* New York, Crown Publishers, Inc.: 1986.

—, *The Black Cat Made Me Buy It!* New York: Crown Publishers, Inc.: 1988.

Necker, Claire. *Four Centuries of Cat Books: A Bibliography, 1570–1970*. Metuchen, New Jersey: The Scarecrow Press, Inc.: 1972.

O'Neill, John P. *Metropolitan Cats*. New York: Metropolitan Museum of Art; Harry N. Abrams, Inc., Publisher: 1981.

Sillar, F. C. and Anne Mobbs. *The Cat Fancier – A Guide to Catland Postcards*. London: Longman: 1982.

Suares, J. C. *The Indispensable Cat*. New York: Stewart, Tabori & Chang, Inc.: 1983.

Tate, Joan. *Cat Country*. Ram Publishing Co.: 1979.

Wilson, Michael. *V and A Cats*. London: Published by the Victoria and Albert Museum: 1989.

CAT COLLECTIONS

England

The British Museum
Great Russel Street, London, WC1B 3DG

The Dyson Perrins Museumn of Worcester Porcelain
Severn Street, Worcester

The Fitzwilliam Museum
Trumpington Street, Cambridge, CB2 1RB

Holly Trees Museum
Colchester, Essex

Mrs. Langton's Cats
The Castle Museum
Norwich, Norfolk, NR1 3JU

The Netherlands

The Cat Cabinet c/o Kika Van Manen
Herengracht 468, 1017 CA Amsterdam

Switzerland

The Cat Museum c/o Rosemarie Muller
Baselstrasse 101, CH-4125 Richen

United States

Abby Aldridge Rockefeller Folk Art Center
307 South England Street, Williamsburg, Virginia, 23185

Beinecke Rare Book and Manuscript Library
Van Vehten-Pollock Cat Collection
Yale University, 1603 University Station, New Haven, Connecticut, 06520

Brooklyn Museum
188 Eastern Parkway, Brooklyn, New York, 11238

Glendale Public Library
222 East Harvard Street, Glendale, California, 91205

Metropolitan Museum of Art
5th Avenue at 82nd Street, New York, 10028

Mr. and Mrs. Frank P. Burnap Collection
The Nelson-Atkins Museum of Arts
4525 Oak Street, Kansas City, Missouri, 64111

COLLECTOR'S CLUB
~
Cat Collectors c/o Marilyn Dipboye 31311 Blair Drive, Warren, Michigan, 48092

PRICE GUIDE

The prices in this guide are retail prices, i.e., what a cat collector who does not own one of these objects will have to pay from a dealer in a middle range antiques mall, shop, or show.

Astute collectors know to comparison shop. If you are willing to work the field and have patience (not an easy requirement for collectors), you can find most objects at prices lower than those appearing in this book

These prices are guides, not absolutes. They are designed to give you an idea of what you might have to pay if you buy on impulse. You decide what you are willing to pay. This is the true price that counts.

Pricing is based upon objects in very good to fine condition. This means that objects can show some signs of wear, albeit not visible at arm's length.

Because of the tremendous interest of cat material that is available, collectors are advised to stress condition when making a purchase.

No.	DESCRIPTION	PROVENANCE	DATE	PRICE
INTRODUCTION				
1	Toy, Cat-in-the-Box	German	1900–1925	$125
2	Figurine, seated cat with two kittens, topaz	Russian	c.1880	$900.00
3	Figurine, two intertwined cats, yin-yang form, jade	Chinese	Possibly 16th C	$3,500.00
4	Book, *Stories About Cats*, Louis Wain (illustrator)	English	1882	$65.00
	Book, *Tales from Catland*, Louis Wain (illustrator)	English	1877 Ed.	$45.00
5	Print, "The Good Puss", Louis Wain (illustrator)	English	Early 20th C	$300.00
6	Sheet Music, The Cat and the Fiddle musical	American	c.1910–20	$25.00
7	Figurine, seated cat, redware	American	1978	$15.00
CERAMIC CATS				
8	Figurine, seated cat, painted redware	Mexican	Contemporary	$15.00
	Figurine, reclining cat, painted redware	Mexican	Contemporary	$10.00
9	Figurine, seated cat, ceramic	Persian	Poss. 17th C	$2,000.00
10	Figurine, seated cat, Meissen, porcelain	German	18th C	$1,250.00
11	Figurine, seated cat on pillow, Staffordshire, ceramic	English	1817–1830	$450.00
12	Figurine, seated cat, Staffordshire, ceramic	English	19th C	$250.00
13	Print, engraving, Gottfried Mind (artist)	English	c.1828	$75.00
14	Figurine, reclining mother cat and kittens, ceramic	English	c.1825–1830	$850.00
15	Figurine, mother cat and kittens, ceramic	English	Early 19th C	$600.00
16	Figurine, seated cat, chalkware	American	1850–1900	$850.00
17	Figurine, seated cat, chalkware	American	1850–1900	$1,000.00
18	Figurines (pair), seated cats, Royal Worcester, porcelain	English	1957	$75.00
19	Figurines (pair), seated cats, porcelain	Thailand	1991	$7.50
20	Figurine group, seated mother cat and playful kitten, bisque	German	Late 19th C	$200.00
21	Figurine, seated cat with paw in air, bisque	German	1920s	$85.00
22	Fairing, Five o'clock Tea	German	c.1890	$185.00
23	Matchholder, ceramic	English	Early 20th C	$55.00
24	(left) Souvenir, heraldic, New Quay	English	Early 20th C	$135.00
	(center) Souvenir, heraldic	English	Early 20th C	$40.00
	(right) Souvenir, heraldic, City of Portsmouth	English	Early 20th C	$100.00
25	(left) Figurine, seated cat with paw in air, porcelain	Japanese	c.1900	$130.00
	(center) Figurine, seated cat with paw in air, porcelain	Japanese	c.1935	$110.00
	(right) Figurine, seated cat with paw in air, porcelain	Japanese	c.1900	$40.00
26	Figurine, seated cat, ceramic, Mike Hinton	English	Contemporary	$12.50
27	Figurine, seated cat, ceramic, Joan and David de Bethel	English	Contemporary	$250.00
28	Figurine, cat running down step, resin, Peter Fagan's *Color Box*	English	Contemporary	$30.00
	Figurine, cat in bathroom, resin, Peter Fagan's *Color Box*	English	Contemporary	$30.00
CATS AS TOYS				
29	Wind-up toy, lithograph tin	Poss. German	Early 20th C	$475.00
30	Counterweight toy, wood	American	1850–1900	$225.00
31	Wind-up toy, lithograph tin	German	Mid-20th C	$150.00
32	Child's rocking toy, wood	American	Mid-20th C	$65.00
33	Push toy, wood	German	c.1969	$50.00
34	Stuffed toy, fabric, Dean's Rag Book Co.	English	c.1925	$40.00
35	Stuffed toy, Steiff	German	Mid-20th C	$165.00
36	Cat nine-pins, Steiff	German	c.1900	$3,000.000
37	Paper panoramic screen, Perry & Co. Limited, London	English	c.1900–1910	$75.00
38	Paper novelty, Raphael Tuck & Sons	English	c.1900–1910	$45.00
39	Game, Kat en Muis, J. Vlieger, Amsterdam	Dutch	c.1900–1925	$200.00
40	Playing card game, Parker Bros.	American	c.1900	$65.00
41	Boxed board game, The Three Little Kittens, Milton Bradley	American	Mid-20th C	$85.00
42	Squeak toy, wood and paper	German	c.1850–1870	$225.00
43	Jigsaw puzzle, Miss Tabby's Party, J. W. Barfoot	English	c.1860	$400.00
44	Jjigsaw puzzle set, The Robber Kittens, Parker Brothers	American	c.1920s	$95.00 Set of 2 $35.00 Single
45	Lantern slides	English	c.1910	$15.00 each
46	Dolls, male and female, Tracey Gallup, Royal Oak, Michigan	American	c.1978	$150.00
	Doll, child, Tracey Gallup, Royal Oak, Michigan	American	c.1981	$120.00
47	Stuffed toy, cloth	Chinese	1960s	$15.00
48	Candlesticks (pair), brass	Austria	1885	$500.00
49	Book, *The Playtime Book*, Ernest Nister (publisher)	English	Early 20th C	$45.00
	Book, *With Louis Wain in Pussyland*, Raphael Tuck (publisher)	English	c.1910	$250.00
50	Figurine, ceramic, Ribby, Beswick	English	Contemporary	$12.00
	Figurine, ceramic, Miss Moppett, Beswick	English	Contemporary	$15.00
51	Stuffed toy, Cat in the Hat, Coleco	American	1983	$15.00
	Book, *Cat in the Hat* autographed by Dr. Seuss	American	1990	$50.00
52	Book, *The White Kitten*, Valentine & Sons (publisher)	English	Mid-20th C	$15.00
53	Jigsaw puzzle set, Saalfield, Fern Bisel Peat (illustrator)	American	Mid-20th C	$65.00

No.	DESCRIPTION	PROVENANCE	DATE	PRICE
54	Cup and Saucer, child's toy set, ceramic, Spode	English	Mid-19th C	$85.00
55	Plate, child's reproduction, Adams	English	1960s	$15.00
	Plate, child's, from "Wireless Set" (tea set), Heathcote China	English	1920s	$45.00 set
56	Plate, child's, earthenware, "The Young Nurses"	English	c.1830–1840	$65.00
57	Mug, child's, ceramic, "The Cat's Bathtime", Louis Wain illustration	English	Early 20th C	$100.00
	Greeting Card, "The Cat's Bathtime", Louis Wain illustration	English	Contemporary	$3.00

CATS AT CHRISTMAS

No.	DESCRIPTION	PROVENANCE	DATE	PRICE
58	Tin, Pat Albeck (illustrator)	Unknown	c.1960s–1970s	$10.00
59	Card, Christmas, published by Hildescheimer & Faulkner	English	c.1880–1890	$15.00
60	Card, Christmas, diecut	Poss. German	c.1900	$12.50
61	Card, Christmas, Mimi Vang Olsen (illustrator)	English	Contemporary	$3.00
62	Ornament, Christmas, blown glass, seated cat	German	1980s	$4.00
	Ornament, Christmas, blown glass, kittens in basket	German	1930s	$12.00
63	Ornament, cat face in relief	Unknown	1980s	$3.00
	Ornament, seated cat, Chinese	Unknown	1980s	$2.00
	Ornament, black cat face, Lesley Homes (illustrator)	Taiwan	1991	$4.00
64	Cake decoration ornaments, bisque	German	c.1920–1930	$15.00 each
	Christmas "cracker" trinkets, small black cats	German	c.1920–1930	$10.00 each
65	Halloween lantern	American	Late 1940s	$65.00
66	Halloween party set	American	c.1950	$45.00
67	Card, birthday, Popshots Inc., Westport, Connecticut	American	1980s	$2.00
68	Calendar, "The Natural Cat Calendar," 1987	American	1987	$5.00
69	Card, Valentine	American	Mid-20th C	$4.00
70	Card, greeting, Lolita, Thaddeus Krumeich (illustrator)	English	c.1980	$2.00

CATS THROUGH THE POST

No.	DESCRIPTION	PROVENANCE	DATE	PRICE
71	Post Card, Maurice Boulanger (French) illustrator	German (printed)	Early 20th C	$10.00
72	Card, "You Are A Dear"	German (printed)	Early 20th C	$4.00
73	Post Card, Louis Wain (illustrator)	English	1906	$12.00
74	Post Card, unknown illustrator	German (printed)	1904	$7.50
75	Post Card, Arthur Thiele (illustrator)	German (printed)	Early 20th C	$5.00
76	Stamps, sheet, Puss-in-Boots	East Germany	1968	$4.00
77	Stamps, plate block, John Dawson (illustrator)	American	1988	$2.50
78	Post Card, S. Sperlich (illustrator)	German (printed)	Early 20th C	$5.00
79	Post Card, "Swing High, Swing Low," Landor	German (printed)	Early 20th C	$3.00
80	Note Card set, issued by National Gallery of Art, Washington DC	American	1986	$15.00
81	Post Card, reproduction, Violet Roberts (illustrator)	English	Contemporary	$1.00
82	Post Card, fold out, Valentine publisher	English	Early 20th C	$5.00
83	Post Card, "Breakfast in Bed Charged Extra"	English	1911	$7.50
84	Post cards, humor	American	1950s	$1.50 each
85	Post card, photo image, cat with felt mouse	German (printed)	c.1910	$5.00
86	Post card, "Out for Luck!," Raphael Tuck	English	c.1925	$4.00

WOODEN CATS

No.	DESCRIPTION	PROVENANCE	DATE	PRICE
87	Doorstop or toy, wood	American	c.1900–1920	$2,500.00+
88	Figurine, wood, dozing cat	Swiss	c.1930s	$90.00
89	Figurine, wood, cat tearing at box containing rat	Japanese	Late 18th C	$10,000.00+
90	Figurine, pearwood, three seated cats with raised paws	Japanese	Late 19th C	$750.00
91	Doorstops or ornaments, wood, painted, made by Natalie Silitch	American	Early 1970s	$15.00 each
92	Figurine, wood, Fat Cat, Pat and Peter Tyber	American	Contemporary	$750.00
93	Figurine, wood, Prairie Cat, Pat and Peter Tyber	American	Contemporary	$250.00
	Figurine, wood, Prairie Kittens, Pat and Peter Tyber	American	Contemporary	$200.00
94	Figurine, wood, dummy board, Maggie Howard (artist)	English	Contemporary	$175.00+ each
95	Nesting Dolls, wood	Chinese	Contemporary	$25.00 each
96	Cat kennel, wood, Sylvia King	English	Contemporary	$25.00

METAL CATS

No.	DESCRIPTION	PROVENANCE	DATE	PRICE
97	Bank, mechanical, metal, Tabby	American	c.1885	$750.00
98	Figurine, seated cat, bronze	Japanese	1980s	$300.00
	Figurine, resting cat, bronze	Japanese	c.1880–1990	$1,500.00
99	Bonbonniere Dish, enamel	English	Late 18th C	$2,500.00
100	Figurine, Austrian bronze, Helen Maguire (designer)	Austrian	1900	$550.00
101	Figurine, pair, Vienese bronze cat bust statues	Austrian	Late 19th C	$150.00
102	Figurine, seated cat, cast pewter and handpainted, Hantel	English	c.1985	$20.00
	Figurine, Puss-in-Boots, cat pewter and handpainted, Hantel	English	c.1985	$25.00
103	Fire-iron holder, seated cat, cast iron	English	Early 20th C	$175.00
104	Ashtray, seated kitten with "Born Blind" sign, brass	English	Mid-20th C	$15.00
105	Bird-scarer, metal	English	Early 20th C	$17.50
	Bird-scarer, metal, marble eyes only	English	Contemporary	$3.00
106	Doll, ceramic head	Taiwan	1980s	$15.00
	Tins, lithographed	English	1980s	$3.00 each
107	Bank, lithographed tin, Kitty Cucumber (illustrator)	Hong Kong	1985	$8.00
	Egg, Easter, lithographed tin, Ian Logan (illustrator)	Switzerland	1980s	$5.00
108	Napkin Ring, silver plated	American	Late 19th C	$350.00

CATS IN TEXTILES

No.	DESCRIPTION	PROVENANCE	DATE	PRICE
109	Needlework, cat's head, embroidery	English	1970s	$275.00
110	Needlework, embroidery, sampler, Sarah Davies	English	Mid-19th C	$850.00

No.	DESCRIPTION	PROVENANCE	DATE	PRICE
111	Woolwork, three-dimensional, cat on pillow	English	c.1880–1920	$625.00
112	Hooked Rug, reclining tabby kitten	American	Early 20th C	$125.00
113	Hooked Rug, sleeping cat	American	Early 20th C	$185.00
114	Quilt, crib, sample block	American	1970s	$50.00 Quilt
115	Quilt Kit, single bed, sample block, Ruth Kortright (sewer)	American	1940s	$250.00 Quilt
116	Handkerchief, tabby kitten, Per Lindstrom (illustrator)	Switzerland	c.1970	$15.00
117	Towel, leaping cat, Kliban (illustrator)	American	c.1980s	$5.00
118	Sewing Bag, Button family illustrated on four sides	American	c.1920	$75.00
	Thimble Holder, bronze, reproduction, Heirloom Editions	American	1984	$25.00
	Thimble, silver, Kay Kendall	English	Contemporary	$35.00
GLASS CATS				
119	Dish, covered, milk glass, Atterbury, Pittsburgh, Pennsylvania	American	Late 19th C	$325.00
120	Dish, covered, milk glass, McKee, Pittsburgh	American	Late 19th C	$145.00
121	Plate, decorative, milk glass, painted, Westmoreland	American	Early 20th C	$85.00
122	Figurine, frosted lead crystal, Lalique, seated cat	French	Mid-20th C	$750.00
123	(left) Figurine, seated cat, Sabino	French	c.1920s	$75.00
	(right) Perfume Bottle, seated cat, black bowtie	Unknown	c.1930s	$45.00
CATS IN ADVERTISING				
124	Cigar Box Label, White Cat	American	Mid-20th C	$25.00
125	Broadside, Nestle's Milk, John Hassall (illustrator)	English	Early 20th C	$125.00
126	Tape Measure, celluloid case	American	Early 20th C	$40.00
127	Poster, London Transport, Horace Taylor (illustrator)	English	1924	$150
128	Trade Card, Frank Knecht	American	Late 19th C	$4.00
129	Match Box, cover is reproduction of late 19th Century trade card	English	Contemporary	$1.00
130	Thread Box, Corticelli	American	Early 20th C	$10.00
131	Jigsaw puzzle, C. I. Hood, Wedding in Catland, Louis Wain (illustrator)	American	c.1890s	$250.00
132	Calendar, Chesapeake & Ohio Railroad, Chessie, 1957	American	1957	$75.00
133	Catalog, Christmas, Fortnum & Mason	English	1958	$45.00
134	Advertising Premium, kite, 9-Lives, Morris the Cat	American	1970s	15.00
KITCHEN CATS				
135	Teapot, ceramic	Japanese	Contemporary	$15.00
136	Butterdish, ceramic	American	1950s	$12.50
137	Candy Mold, pewter, T. Mills, Philadelphia, Pennsylvania	American	Early 20th C	$85.00 each
138	Tray, serving, lithographed tin, Lesley Anne Ivory (illustrator)	English	Contemporary	$8.00
139	Hot Pad, cloth, Woodchips Designers	American	1980s	$3.00
140	Plate and Mug set, six designs, issued by British National Trust	English	Contemporary	$20.00
141	Glass Mugs, McDonald's fast food premium	American	1980s	$3.00 each
142	Bowl, enamel, Mikkimugs, Edward Lear (illustrator)	English	1988	$8.00
143	Can Opener, seated cat	Hong Kong	Contemporary	$10.00
144	(top) Stringholder, ceramic	Unknown origin	Mid-20th C	$25.00
	(bottom) Stringholder, ceramic, Babbacombe Pottery	English	Mid-20th C	$20.00
145	Mustard Pot, ceramic	German	Late 19th C	$55.00
146	Refrigerator Magnet, Halloween witch cat, wood	American	1980s	$3.00
147	Salt and Pepper Shakers (pair), Shawnee	American	c.1940–50	$12.00
CHARACTER CATS				
148	Hot Water Bottle, Sylvester and Tweety	Spanish	Mid-20th C	$65.00
149	Bath Soap Bottle, Felix the Cat	American	1980s	$15.00 each
150	Walking Toy, stuffed, Felix the Cat	English	c.1920s–1930s	$500.00
151	Walker, wood, homemade, Felix the Cat	American	Mid-20th C	$125.00
152	Comic Book, "Land of the Flying Carpets," Felix the Cat, Harvey	American	1958	$8.00
153	Jigsaw Puzzle, frame tray, Percy Puzz, Fairchild Corp.	American	1950s	$20.00
154	Sheet Music, Sylvester and Tweety	American	Mid-20th C	$25.00
155	Hot Water Bottle, Tom and Jerry	Spanish	Mid-20th C	$65.00
156	Pinback Button, Fritz the Cat	American	1960s	$5.00
157	Pez Containers, Arlene, Nermel, and Garfield	Austrian	1980s	$2.00 each
158	Bath Soap Bottle, Mr. Jinks and Pixie and Dixie, Hanna Barbera	American	1960s	$18.00
159	Bath Soap Bottles, Punkin Puss and Mush Mouse, Hanna Barbera	American	1960s	$20.00 each
160	Little Golden Book, Ruff and Reddy, Ann McGovern author	American	1959	$15.00
161	Bath Soap Bottle, Top Cat, Hanna Barbera	American	1960s	$15.00
VARIOUS CATS				
162	Photograph, Museum of Miniature Furniture, Normandy, France	French	Contemporary	FREE
162	Figurine, ceramic, reproduction, Egyptian, British Museum	English	Contemporary	$15.00
163	Poster, Louis Wain exhibition	English	1973	$15.00
165	Brooch, plastic, Amiee Bananee	American	1989	$25.00
166	Badge, "Sans Peur," Scottish	English	20th C	$75.00
167	Brooch, rhinestone, seated cat	English	1950s	$35.00
168	Brooch, enamel, three cats under lamp post	Unknown	1930s	$50.00
169	Brooch, silver, seated cat, G. Iaffi	Peruvian	Late 20th C	$40.00
170	Brooch, silvered metal, cat at rest, Art Deco	French	c.1930s	$20.00
171	Brooch, silver, cat in front of fireplace, Philip Isern (artist)	English	c.1987	$45.00
172	Soap, curled cat, wicker basket	English	1980s	$5.00
173	Sheet Music, "Kitten on the Keys"	American	Early 20th C	$10.00
175	Thimbles, ceramic	Unknown	Contemporary	$15.00 each
176	Hot Water Bottle, rubber	Unknown	Contemporary	$5.00

INDEX

Numbers in italics refer to illustrations.

A
animaliers, French 11, 72, 76

B
Black Cat magazine 41–2
black cats 42, 50, 51, *51*, *61*, *62*, 78, 93, 95–6, 102, 106, *120*, 123
Boettcher, Sue 78, 102
books *10*, 11, 38, 39, 41, 118
  children's 12, 30, 38, *39*, 41
  comic 108, *110*, 112, 116, *116*
  illustrated 38–41
brass *38*, 72, 76, *76*
bronze 11, 46, 72, *72*, 73–4, *73*, *74*, 75, 76, 86
Burnap collection 9, 17

C
calendars 47, 50, 52, *52*
cardboard 31, *31*, 32, 96, 98
cards, Christmas 11, 30, 46–8, 58
  greeting *52*, 53, *53*, *54*, *56*, 85
  photographic 59–61, 59
  note 60
  (*see also* postcards)
carousel cats 70
cartoon cats 12, 27, *94*, 102, *103*, 107–116
cast-iron *71*, 72, 75–76, *75*, *76*
cat dolls 28, 37, *37*, *40*
  nesting 69, *69*
Cat and Fiddle *12*, 24, 36, 43, 122
cat food 98, *98*
cat games 30, 32–4, *32*
  American 33–4, *34*
cat houses 69–70, *70*
Cat in the Hat 28, *40*, 41
Cat Museum, Basel 118
ceramics 12, *12*, 14–24, *22*, *23*, *99*, 101, 102, *102*, 103, 104, *104*, 118
  children's 24, 42–4, *43*, *44*, 108
  porcelain 9, 14, *14*, 15, *15*, *16*, 18–19, *18*, *19*, 21, 22, *22*, *39*
  to identify 16–17
Cheshire Cat 19, 58, 78, 116
Chessie and Peake 81, 97, *97*
chimney boards 66–7, 68
Christmas:
  cards 11, 30, 46–8, *46*, *47*, *48*, 58
  catalogs 97
  decorations 48–50, *48*, *49*, *50*
comic *see* books
containers *73*, 77, *77*, 78, *78*, 93, 94, 102, *113*, *115*

D
de Bethel cats 22, *23*
diaries 50, 52
dolls' house items 24, 42, 43
domestic objects 9, *21*, *38*, 72, 75, *75*, 78, *78*, 85, 86, *86*, *93*, 99–106, *99*, *100*, *101*, *102*, *103*, *104*, *105*, *106*, *107*, *112*, 122, *122*, 123, *123*
dummy boards 65–6, 68, *68*

E
embroidery 88, *80*, 81–2, *81*
enamel signs 96
enamelled objects 72, 73, *73*, 103, *103*
exhibitions 12, 64–5, 89, 118

F
fabrics, printed 28, *28*, 83, 85, *85*, 101–2
fairings 20, *20*
Felix 12, 27, *94*, 108, *108*, *109*, 110, *110*

G
Gallé cats 19, 22
Garfield 102, *102*, 108, 113, *113*
glass 88–90, *88*, *89*, *90*

H
Hanna-Barbera cartoon cats 111, 112, *112*, 114, *114*, 115, 116, *116*
Herbert, Susan 52, 53, 94
Holmes, Lesley *49*, 85, 101

I
Ivory, Lesley Anne 48, 77, 100–1, *101*, 123

J
jewelry 72, 120, *120*
jigsaws 30, 34, 35, *35*, 41, *42*, *96*, *110*, 112

L
lace 86
Lalique cats 89, *89*
Langton collection 8, 14, 15, 16, 64
Lear, Edward 58, 103, *103*
Leman, Martin 39, 48, 49

M
magazines 41, 47, 98
magic-lantern slides 12, 36–7, *36*
Maguire, Helena 38, *39*, 46, 47, 48, 58, 59, *73*
Mind, Gottfried 16, *16*, 43

museum exhibits 8, 9, 14, 18, 28, 34–5, 66–7, 69, 70, 74–5, 80, 81, 83, 118–9

N
Nister, Ernest (publisher) 38–9, *39*, 52, 56, 78

P
papier-mâché 22, 34, 93
perfume bottles *15*, 89, *90*
photographs 59, *59*, 60–1, 69, 70, *117*
pewter *74*, 75, 76, *76*
porcelain *see* ceramics
postage stamps 11, 58, *58*
postcards 55–62, *55*, *57*, *59*, *60*, *61*, *62*, 118
  novelty 62, *62*
posters 94, *94*, 116, 118, *119*
Potter, Beatrix 39, *39*, 78, 85
prints 11, *11*, 96, 118
Puss in Boots 24, 31, 36, 38, *38*, 58, *58*, *74*, 75, 100, *106*

Q
quilts 84, *84*

R
rugs 81–3, *82*, *83*

S
Sabino cats 89, *90*
samplers 80–1, *80*
scraps 9, 30

sheet music *12*, *111*, 122, *122*
silver 50, 78, *78*, *86*
souvenirs, heraldic 20–1, *21*

T
Thiele, Arthur 57, *57*, 58
tiles 106, 118–9
tins, decorated *45*, 77–8, 93, 94, 102
toys 7, 9, 12, 26–44, *25*, *26*, *27*, *28*, *29*, *31*, *34*
  paper 30–2
  stuffed 28, *28*, *29*, *40*, 86, *108*
  tinplate *25*, *26*, 27
  wooden *27*, 34, 64, 69, *109*
trade cards 95, *95*, 123
trade marks *91*, 95–6
Tuck, Raphael 30–2, *30*, *31*, *39*, 46, 52, 56, 58–9, 61, *61*, *62*, *62*
Tyber Katz 67, *67*

W
Wain, Louis 10, 11, *11*, 12, 23–4, 38, 39, *39*, 44, *44*, 47, 48, 56, 57, *57*, 58, 61, 93, 94, 97, 118, *119*
wallpaper 12, 39, 66, 119, 122
Weir, Harrison 10, *10*, 38, 100
where to find items 12, 19, 21, 27, 28, 34, 35, 36, 48, 103, 104, 118
Whieldon, Thomas 17–18
Winstanley cats 22
wooden cats *27*, 34, 63–70, *63*, *64*, *65*, *66*, *68*
  toys *27*, 34, 64, 69, *109*
wrapping paper 53–4

ACKNOWLEDGEMENTS
~

The publishers would like to extend thanks to the following individuals for generously offering items in their collections to be photographed:

Anna M. Benner, Emmaus, Pennsylvania; Patricia M. Carrigan, Bay City, Michigan; Faith Eaton; Pauline Flick; Roselyn Gerson, Malverne, New York; Gwen Goldman, Adamstown, Pennsylvania; Charles Gottschall, Philadelphia, Pennsylvania; Mrs. Graham Greene; Maggie Howard; Connie A. Moore, Zionsville, Pennsylvania; Harry L. Rinker, Zionsville, Pennsylvania; Julie Pelletier Robinson, Easton, Pennsylvania; John and Mildred Spear, Manheim, Pennsylvania; Richie and Sue Sternfeld, Glendale, New York; Ellery Yale Wood.

Special thanks to: Marilyn Dipboye, Cat Collectors, Warren, Michigan.

PICTURE CREDITS
~

London Transport Museum: p94; Norfolk Museums Service (Norwich Castle Museum): pp85t and b, 14t and b, 15t, 16t, 16br, 64t, 65, 73t; Ohio Historical Society: pp25, 71, 87, 88t, 100b; The Washington Doll's House and Toy Museum: pp33, 74; The Weycroft Collection: p64b.